Action Learning
in Social Work

Paula

I wish you all the best in
your final year of studies!

All the best,

Paul

Action Learning in Social Work

CHRISTINE ABBOTT
AND PAUL TAYLOR

Series Editors: Steven Keen and Keith Brown

Los Angeles | London | New Delhi
Singapore | Washington DC

Learning Matters
An imprint of SAGE Publications Ltd
1 Oliver's Yard
55 City Road
London EC1Y 1SP

SAGE Publications Inc.
2455 Teller Road
Thousand Oaks, California 91320

SAGE Publications India Pvt Ltd
B 1/I 1 Mohan Cooperative Industrial Area
Mathura Road
New Delhi 110 044

SAGE Publications Asia-Pacific Pte Ltd
3 Church Street
#10–04 Samsung Hub
Singapore 049483

Editor: Luke Block
Development editor: Lauren Simpson
Production controller: Chris Marke
Project management: Swales & Willis Ltd,
Exeter, Devon
Marketing manager: Tamara Navaratnam
Cover design: Wendy Scott
Typeset by: C&M Digitals (P) Ltd, Chennai,
India
Printed and bound by Henry Ling Limited,
at the Dorset Press, Dorchester, DT1 1HD

Library of Congress Control Number:
2013940926

British Library Cataloguing in Publication
Data

A catalogue record for this book is available
from the British Library

MIX
Paper from
responsible sources
FSC
www.fsc.org **FSC® C013985**

ISBN 978-1-4462-7534-4
ISBN 978-1-4462-7535-1 (pbk)

Contents

List of figures

List of tables

Foreword

All texts in the Post-Qualifying Social Work series have been written by people with a passion for excellence in social work practice. They are primarily written to help social work practitioners in their day-to-day roles but they will also be useful for any social worker undertaking more formal professional development.

As the books in this series are written by practitioners, they will also be of value to social work students as they are designed to inform, inspire and develop social work practice.

We trust you will find this text of real value to your practice as a social worker and that this, in turn, has a real impact on those we serve.

Dr Steven Keen and Professor Keith Brown
National Centre for Social Work, Bournemouth University

About the authors

Christine Abbott is an action learning practitioner, author and academic. She is an associate of the Open University, facilitating undergraduate and postgraduate modules. Christine is a partner in the Centre for Action Learning Facilitation (C-ALF) which is partnering with Skills for Care UK to support action learning in social work. Christine works internationally in both the public and private sectors and is the co-author of the qualification standards for action learning facilitation. Christine is interested in the development of leaders and managers and is a former chairman and current non-executive director and trustee of the Institute of Leadership and Management.

Paul Taylor currently works for Southend Borough Council as a lead social worker for NHS Continuing Healthcare and ASYE Manager for adult services. Paul is also an associate lecturer for the University of Essex and an associate with the Centre for Action Learning Facilitation (C-ALF). Paul has a strong interest in emotional and social intelligence, transactional analysis and critical analysis and reflection. In his spare time, he enjoys training for and competing in middle- and long-distance triathlon and marathon-distance races.

Acknowledgements

We would like to acknowledge the many social workers who contributed with their ideas and experiences of action learning to the writing of this book.

Thanks also to Roger and Jess – our own personal 'comrades in adversity'.

Introduction

Christine and Paul met in 2010 on a programme to support practice educators and social work managers in facilitating action learning to support newly qualified social workers. Skills for Care had commissioned Christine to deliver the programme and Paul was a participant. It was a challenging start – Paul thought that he was attending a mentoring programme for newly qualified social workers and was not convinced this programme would meet his needs.

It was during this programme and subsequently when Paul's curiosity was sufficiently aroused that he attended the follow-up Institute of Leadership and Management Certificate in Action Learning facilitation. With Christine and Mike Pedler, co-director of the Centre for Action Learning Facilitation, conversations developed around the similarity between the principles of action learning and social work practice. They both have at their heart real-time problem solving, getting things done and critical reflection. Skills for Care are promoting action learning as a method of developing critical practitioners, and so this book was born.

We will argue in this book that action learning methodology has strong links with social work problem solving. There are high levels of risk, uncertainty and change in the public sector and, in particular, social work, that require an approach that questions perspective and assumptions and allows workers to feel challenged in a supportive environment as 'comrades in adversity'. The key focus in this book is on critical reflective practice and the action learning approach that aims to empower, support deep learning and promote emotional and social 'intelligence'.

Understanding action learning is a problem in itself, and in this book we have tried both to explain the simplicity and retain the moral purpose of the process or way of working. Reg Revans, the founder of action learning, in his writings reveals the profound nature and often mystery by citing the Bible, Koran and the teachings of Buddha as evidence that the idea is an old one, yet at the same time insisting that it is needed today as a new approach to working and learning.

Action learning involves doing something other than what you are currently doing; learning from real problems in real time means that you are constantly challenging the current norms and operating assumptions of the organisation and your own practice as a social worker. You will see that the purpose of working in an action learning set is to 'rock the boat' of your current thinking, and to reframe the problems you face as a result of the 'way we do things around here'. Those things may lead to good outcomes but action learning helps to uncover the shadow side of the wicked problems. So, for example, you may be in an organisation that uses key performance indicators that focus your energy on those aspects of your work that are measurable, but that very system may result in a lack of quality. Most, if not all, of you will lead busy working lives spent *doing* things – after all, that's what you are paid to do – but have little time or space for critical reflection, to question *what* you are doing, why you are doing it and challenge yours and others' assumptions. We aim to show how, by creating both time and space, through action learning, people develop themselves and build the relationships that are the key to improving their practice.

> *The action learning set gave me the rare opportunity to get out of the fast flowing river of practice, where I was often in the rapids, bouncing off the rocks, and sit on the river bank and reflect on life in the river, to observe from a distance the problems I faced. That permission to be open, share, challenge and support in a confidential setting created both individual and collective learning. It allowed me to learn and develop as a practitioner and as a person.*

(Social worker)

Like action learning, social work is difficult to define and, whether working with children, adults, families or a combination of each of these groups, it's a complex and tricky task to get right. With such complexity in environments of uncertainty and risk, action learning can support the development of ethical and critical practitioners who can support one another in the relative safety of a learning set. In the social work context, action learning can support practitioner development, including emotional intelligence, anti-oppressive practice and critical reflection, all of which are highly desirable for individuals, teams and organisations attempting to keep up with the rate of external change. It is particularly helpful in multi-agency settings to break down the barriers between departments and professions and seek to develop further the inventiveness and innovativeness of practice. Social work also has its roots in morality, challenging social injustice, and clear codes of ethics and values of practice, including anti-discriminatory practice and emancipation, to name just a few of the areas of practice. Social work also has a person-centred ethos and as you begin your journey through this book, you will be able to identify that action learning also has this underlying principle to support each other in times of adversity.

This is a practical book to support you in the development, through action learning, as a critically reflective practitioner. In each chapter we introduce ideas and concepts and we encourage you to reflect on these in the context of your own practice and find ways of sharing your ideas with others. We provide you with resources that will help you, including the Centre for Action Learning Facilitation website, where you can share your reflections with other action learning participants and facilitators.

The book is written in three parts.

Part 1: Principles – Chapters 1–3 provide an introduction to action learning, social work and action learning and critical reflection in action learning.

Part 2: Context – Chapters 4–7 introduce you specifically to action learning in social work and then where action learning can have a specific impact.

Part 3: Practice – Chapters 8 and 9 are written for those who have been invited to become a member of an action learning set and those who are asked to facilitate or would be interested in a facilitation role.

Part 1: Principles

Chapter 1 Action learning: an introduction

This chapter introduces the principles of action learning proposed by its originator, Reg Revans. It covers Revans's early influences, both personal and professional, in the formation of the principles and practices of action learning. We discuss the various approaches today, modes of learning and the relationship between action learning and social work practice education and supervision. We introduce the notion that through action learning we can all generate and act on knowledge rather than passively accepting the results of research produced by experts. This chapter in particular links to the 'Ethics and Values' domain of the Professional Capabilities Framework (PCF) and will help you to reflect on your capabilities as a social worker to recognise your values and those of others, including social work as a profession.

Chapter 2 Action learning and social work

This chapter explores the relationship between social work and action learning. Social work has a requirement to perform well in areas of problem solving in real time and in real-life situations to achieve positive outcomes for service users. The performance agenda is still high on the priority list for social workers, managers and directors alike; however, it is simply not enough for statistics and other quantitative measures to realise fully the potential for social work and for other and, arguably, more important outcomes to be met with service users, carers and families. This requires a different approach to how we work, not just with service users, but with other professional groups and in our own teams. This chapter will give an introduction to, and overview of, some of the contemporary and fundamental issues facing social work students, social workers and managers, including issues of stress, decision making, supervision, change, reflective practice and social work identity. These issues will be explored together with how action learning as a methodology can support your social work practice. In terms of the PCF, the domains of 'Professionalism', 'Knowledge' and 'Critical Reflection and Analysis' are covered in this chapter, which will help you to recognise, reflect and analyse some of the core issues in professional social work practice.

Chapter 3 Action learning and critically reflective practice

This chapter introduces the idea of critically reflective practice within action learning. It argues that there is a need to question assumptions about what is prescribed as 'good practice' and the evidence base, which underpins assessment and inter- ventions with service users/carers. The action learning methodology is highlighted as helpful in supporting social workers to reflect critically on their practice within a wider social and professional context. It considers the notion of the social worker as a 'tempered radical' championing emancipation for service users and the profession. As The College of Social Work (2012) highlights, *critical reflection entails insight, exploratory and creative thinking for each unique piece of prac- tice* and, importantly, *over time, social work practitioners should become highly skilled in this*. The chapter supports your capabilities under the 'Critical Reflection and Analysis' domain and there is an emphasis on what it means to be 'critical' in action learning and social work – terms which are often difficult to define and poorly understood by practitioners.

Part 2: Context

Chapter 4 Social and emotional intelligence

This chapter sets out a rationale for action learning having a key role in promot- ing social workers' abilities to understand themselves and others in different ways and step outside of their realities to work as *comrades in adversity*. The chapter will have a focus on the brain (and some neuroscience) to develop your understanding on how the brain works at a more biochemical and physiological level and there will be an overview of some of the key areas of the brain involved with emotion and cognition (feeling and thinking). The ideas of *thinking, feel- ing* and *willing (action)* are discussed which demonstrate that the action learning methodology allows practitioners to question insight at different levels of con- sciousness. It is argued that this will aid the social work intervention (especially in assessment) with service users and families as practitioners become more com- petent and capable of working in group environments, e.g. with families. Stress in social work will be discussed as a theme and how action learning sets can sup- port practitioners in times of uncertainty, change and when feeling anxious or stressed with the difficult social work role. Furthermore, becoming socially and emotionally intelligent is explored, including the very basics and complexities of building rapport, and relationships between social workers and service users. The PCF domains of 'Intervention Skills' and 'Professionalism' are covered in this chapter, particularly addressing the need for social workers to 'promote well- being at work' and 'maintaining professionalism in the face of challenge'.

Chapter 5 Anti-discriminatory practice and anti-oppressive practice

In England, both the General Social Care Council and lately the Health and Care Professions Council have highlighted both of these practices as being key to social work practice. Taking part in action learning allows social workers to challenge all sorts of issues of power and discrimination at the personal and at the wider organisation level. This chapter links well to Chapter 3 and will support your developing confidence in challenging inequity and social injustice. It is argued that this is a fundamental skill for social workers to develop and practise, whether this is in the workplace, with other health and social work professionals or in the wider community. It is not surprising to learn that 'Diversity' is one of the nine capabilities on the PCF recently introduced to England and which requires social workers to challenge inequity, marginalisation and power imbalances appropriately. Linked with Chapter 3 and throughout the book, the power of questioning, reflexivity and different types of power are explored in this chapter to dig into the world of anti-oppressive and anti-discriminatory practice, all to take the practitioner further towards the core of becoming 'critical'.

Chapter 6 Involving other professions: multi-agency practice

This chapter has a focus on the importance of building professional relationships across disciplines. It will include practice examples of how this has operated in previous action learning sets and some of the findings, pitfalls and opportunities in building relationships with health and social care practitioners. The advantages of undertaking action learning and cross-pollinating ideas, thinking, feeling and action across disciplines are exciting areas to get involved in. In adult social work practice, hospital social work practitioners may well benefit from engaging their health counterparts in working through problems and issues related to the timely and safe discharge of service users from acute care. Similarly, children and adult community social work practitioners might equally benefit from working in sets with the police, health colleagues and other allied health professionals to develop action plans for promoting protection, safety and independence in the community. In either case, the use of action learning sets is one way to develop appropriate professional relationships where problem solving, decision making and critical reflection can occur across the health and social care interface – particularly relevant in England with recent NHS reforms. Working with others is a core tenet of the PCF and is explored through several domains, including 'Professionalism' and, in particular, 'Contexts and Organisations'.

Chapter 7 Case studies: action learning sets in action

This chapter brings together the experiences of action learning sets at different levels, including individual, team, organisation and multi-agency, to demonstrate action learning in practice. It includes a summary of how action learning was implemented through to the challenges and opportunities that were faced by set members, teams and the organisation. The case studies will support the synthesis of the principles and practice of action learning in various contexts, and allow for reflection on your own experiences that are related to these real-life cases. This chapter will integrate some of the principles and contexts learnt throughout

Parts 1 and 2 and will help support your continuous professional development evidence in a number of domains under the PCF.

Part 3: Practice

Chapter 8 Being an action learner

This chapter is a very practical chapter that introduces the reader to the requirements of being a set member and what a social work practitioner can expect when joining an action learning set. Listening and questioning skills in reflection and action will be explored. The role of the set facilitator will be explained, as well as the methods that facilitators might employ to support the set member (links to Chapter 9). Additionally, the skills of set membership that are required with both self-managed action learning sets and virtual action learning sets will be considered. 'Testing new approaches' is highlighted under the 'Professional Leadership' domain on the PCF and using action learning as a new approach to developing yourself and others will demonstrate this area of practice.

Chapter 9 Facilitating action learning

Facilitation in action learning can be helpful for those sets that need an injection of enthusiasm and support in modelling appropriate questions to set members and also to keep the set on track. The chapter will establish three key roles of the facilitator: the 'accoucheur' or initiator, the 'combiner' and the facilitator of organisational learning. These roles, described by Pedler and Abbott (2013), highlight that facilitation is not always preferred. However, it is argued that facilitation can support action learning sets provided that the facilitator becomes acutely aware of his or her power and influence and learns not to become a teacher. There will be links between adult learning theory and the need for set members to become self-directed in their learning and continuous professional development. The PCF has highlighted the necessity for social work practitioners to *demonstrate professional commitment by taking responsibility for their conduct, practice and learning, with support through supervision.* Similar to Chapter 8, this chapter will facilitate your development to enhance your practice and that of others by using action learning as a methodology in your social work practice.

Part 1
Principles

Chapter 1
Action learning: an introduction

PROFESSIONAL CAPABILITIES FRAMEWORK

This chapter will help you demonstrate the following capabilities:

- Ethics and Values 2.2 – Recognise and, with support, manage the impact of own values on professional practice.
- Critical Reflection and Analysis 6.3 – With support, rigorously question and evaluate the reliability and validity of information from different sources.
- Professional Leadership 9.2 – Recognise the value of, and contribute to, supporting the learning and development of others.

Introduction

This chapter introduces the principles of action learning as proposed by its originator, Reg Revans. It covers Revans's early influences, both personal and professional, in the formation of the principles and practices of action learning. We discuss the various approaches today, modes of learning and the relationship between action learning and social work practice education and supervision. We introduce the notion that through action learning we can all generate and act on knowledge rather than passively accepting the results of research produced by experts.

Revans is considered to be the father of action learning; however, in his extensive writing on the subject he never provided a definitive statement and, as Mumford (1995) noted, he alternated the emphasis regularly. However, what Revans did do was explain his ideas behind the concept:

> *The central idea of this approach to human development, at all levels, in all cultures and for all purposes is, today, that of a set, or small group of comrades in adversity, striving to learn with and from each other as they confess failures and expand victories . . .*

(Revans, 1980)

In all Revans's writings it is evident that he intended action learning to be a deeper, more revolutionary process than other pedagogical models. He intended it to be more than 'learning by doing' and posited the argument that learning is

9

about individual and organisational development and as such it contains within it a moral philosophy involving a number of factors.

Honesty about oneself

Revans spent time in Belgium on an action learning programme where the top managers were asked what was the most valuable question they had learned – the answer was 'What is an honest man, and what do I need to become one?'

Wanting to achieve something good in the world

Revans often uses quotes from the Bible, Koran, Buddha and philosophers to illustrate the point:

> *But be doers of the word, and not only hearers of it, blinding yourselves with false ideas.*

> (Letter of St James, Chapter 1 verses 22–25 AD 60 in Revans, 1983)

> *To do a little good is better than to write difficult books. The perfect man is nothing if he does not diffuse benefits on other creatures, if he does not console the lonely. The way of salvation is open to all, but know that a man deceives himself if he thinks he can escape his conscience by taking refuge in a monastery. The only remedy for evil is healthy reality.*

> (Buddha in Revans, 1980: 13)

> *We ought to do our neighbour all the good we can. If you do good, good will be done to you: but if you do evil, the same will be measured back to you again.*

> (Bidpai, Panchatantra c.326 BC in Revans, 1980: 141)

For friendship

Revans (1983) cites John Macmurray in 'The self' as agent as the ultimate purpose of the action learning moral philosophy:

> *All meaningful knowledge is for the sake of action, and all meaningful action for the sake of friendship.*

Revans's ideas challenge current views of management and learning. Action learning's aim of an upward communication of doubt, in the belief that the doubt ascending speeds up wisdom from above, is an ambitious vision. A colleague of ours remarks cynically that in some organisations it is more like *doubt ascending speeds up retribution from above*!

Revans used the quotation from Buddha, above, to summarise the educational needs of our times. Pedler summarises the definition and assumption of action learning as a pedagogical approach thus:

Action learning is an approach to the development of people in organisations which takes the task as the vehicle for learning. It is based on the premise that there is no learning without action and no sober and deliberate action without learning. On the whole, our education system has not been based upon this principle. The method has been pioneered in work organisations and has three main components – people, who accept the responsibility for taking action on a particular issue; problems or the tasks that people set themselves; and a set of six or so colleagues who support and challenge each other to make progress on problems. Action on a problem changes both the problem and the person acting upon it. It proceeds particularly by questioning taken-for-granted knowledge.

(Pedler, 1997: xxii–xxiii)

Described as a method of 'small group learning', Gaunt emphasised action learning as being:

the art of development – development of problems into opportunities and of people from what they are now to what they may become potentially.

(Gaunt, 1991)

More recently, it has been described by McGill and Brockbank as:

A continuing process of learning and reflection with the support of a group of colleagues, working on real issues . . . [it] can achieve improvement and transformation in a wide range of applications and disciplines including professional, training and other contexts.

(McGill and Brockbank, 2006)

The origin of action learning ideas

Action learning comes from a strong value base and is seen by many as a way of working – even a philosophy. There appear to be a number of key events in the early life of Revans that shaped his ideas of learning and development. His father was a naval architect and was engaged in the investigation of the sinking of the Titanic in 1912. He recalls how his father heard stories from sailors who had tried to warn the authorities of the risks involved and how these risks were ignored. He remembers his father telling him that what he learned during the investigation process was the need to value all views regardless of hierarchy for it was here that the distinction between cleverness and wisdom could be found. In this context he learned from his father the importance of seeking understanding, not just knowledge.

Revans was a member of the Society of Friends or Quakers. The Quakers are a society of equals and therefore do not have a clergy. Often in Revans's writings there are references to ethical values and principles, a desire for social harmony and respect for others' views, honesty and social responsibility. His work today may indeed be termed as promoting inclusivity and participation. Boshyk and Dilworth (2010) draw the comparison of the Quaker practice of the clearness committee and action learning sets. The clearness committee is a communal approach to problem resolution. It starts with the principle that, when we face a problem that is ours to resolve, the inner resources are present but often obscured by layers of interference. The clearness committee works by a person calling a group of diverse people whom they trust to help them become clear with honest authentic, challenging loving questions. Crucially in terms of action learning, it prohibits advice.

Later, when he was a research scientist at the Cavendish Laboratory (1928–1935), Revans describes how at the research seminars fellow researchers were encouraged and became skilled at describing their ignorance and trading that ignorance with others. He found the process of questioning each other in a precise deliberate way and reflecting on the ignorance together helped all present to gain insights on their research. Revans left the Cavendish Laboratory when it became apparent that there was military interest in the work being carried out on splitting the atom.

In 1944, Revans joined the newly nationalised coal industry where he was employed to be responsible for education and training. His first reaction was to spend time as a miner working at the coalface with experienced miners who were well educated in the harsh reality of coal extraction. Apart from not assuming knowledge about something he had never experienced, he noticed how reliant each miner was on the other for safety and teamwork, which reminded him of the work at the Cavendish Laboratory. Revans believed that individual colliery managers could use the methods from the Cavendish Laboratory to come up with creative solutions to problems, without the need for experts and lecturers. He noted that learning was more productive when it came out of mutual enquiry, allowing managers to question their own experience and reflect on their own actions in relation to their current challenge.

Revans sums up his experience thus:

> To most servants of the Coal Board in 1950, as the National Health Service today, the key to successful re-organisation has nothing to do with the capacity of its employees to learn from their experiences of success and failure; it is still a matter of the 'right' central plans fed into the 'right' administrative structure.

(Revans, 1980: 23)

Revans became a Professor of Industrial Administration (now would be known as management) in the UK, a position he held at Manchester University for ten years. After becoming increasingly dissatisfied with an education system that he believed focused too much on the input of knowledge with little reference to practice, he resigned and concentrated on developing the practice of action learning.

REFLECTION POINT

- *Where do your ideas about learning stem from?*

- *How do those ideas reflect your own values?*

- *How do you act on those values in supporting your, others' and organisational and professional learning?*

Since Revans's articulation of the notion of action learning, it has been applied throughout the world (Smith and O'Neil, 2003), including in the UK in organisations as large as the NHS through to groups of sheep farmers in rural Wales. In the field of social work a number of approaches to action learning have been utilised (Table 1.1); however, all are based on the principle that action learning is learning through experience, with the task, and the problem or challenge being the vehicle for learning.

Table 1.1 Approaches to action learning

Characteristics

Face-to-face set meetings with members from different organisations or roles within an organisation, each bringing their own problem or challenge to the meeting

Each member works on tackling an ongoing 'problem' of their own – that is, a challenge or initiative that has hitherto not been solved

Participants describe their projects and proposed action. Others provide challenge and support. Issues such as power, voice, risk, purpose and conflict are overtly brought into the open and explored

Face-to-face set meetings where each member of the set has a similar role. The problems and challenges brought to the set are concerned with this role/or professional theme

Each member works on tackling an ongoing 'problem' of their own – that is, a challenge or initiative that has hitherto not been solved but in the context of the common role

Participants describe their projects and proposed action. Others provide challenge and support. Issues such as power, voice, risk, purpose and conflict are overtly brought into the open and explored

Virtual action learning

There are two main types:

Synchronous: All group members are connected at the same time – usually by telephone, Skype or similar. Meetings are held every 4–8 weeks

Asynchronous: Using discussion boards and forums, participants join in at times to suit themselves and their circumstances. Contributions are made at times to suit each participant

Both of these can be very useful and cost-effective when participants are geographically widespread

---

Smith and O'Neil (2003), Bannan-Ritland (2003), Dotlich and Noel (1998), Yorks *et al.* (1999) and Marquardt (2004) all identify a number of key characteristics that are common:

- real problems or challenges with no 'right' answer that are relevant to the participants' work and of importance to the group or individual;
- happens in real time;
- participants meet over a period of time in groups of preferably diverse backgrounds or organisations of approximately six;
- a process that focuses on questions, reflection and learning;
- an individual, team and organisational commitment to learning;
- participants have the power to take action between set meetings to resolve the problem;
- a set facilitator who captures the learning and improves the process.

Action learning principles

Revans's ecological formula $L \geq C$

Revans suggests that people and organisations cannot survive unless their rate of learning (L) is equal to, or greater than, the rate of change (C) being experienced. We live in an era of rapid change and people and organisations that are unable to sense and respond to those changes are soon in trouble. A negative response to change is to do more of what we learned yesterday in the hope it will work today. Revans argued that a positive response to change is achieved by learning to do tomorrow what might have been unnecessary today.

Revans's formula for learning $L = P + Q$

Learning (L) has two elements – traditional instruction or programmed knowledge (P) and critical reflection or questioning insight (Q). This gives the learning equation $L = P + Q$.

Revans explains:

> *P is the concern of the traditional academy; Q is the field of action learning . . . On the whole, however, programmed knowledge, P, already set out in books or known to expert authorities, is quite insufficient for keeping on top of a world like ours today, racked by change of every kind. Programmed knowledge must not only be expanded; it must be supplemented by questioning insight, the capacity to identify useful and fresh lines of enquiry. This we may denote by Q, so that learning means*

not only supplementing P but developing Q as well. It is arguable which is more important in 1984; the evidence is that a surfeit of P inhibits Q, and that experts, loaded with P, are the greatest menace to adaptation to change by questioning, Q.

(Revans, 1984: 16)

Revans does not dismiss the need for programmed knowledge, or the views of those who rely on such knowledge for their expertise. However, he recognises that the difficulty of reliance on the expert in practice is that it assumes that future issues are almost identical to the ones the expert encountered and that therefore programmed knowledge will work. However, as we have already said, most 'wicked problems' are context-specific and unique; and therefore what worked somewhere else will not work here, due to the people, power and politics. If we take the world of social work practice as being constantly changing, reliance on programmed knowledge on practice and organising practice could become a fatal weakness for the profession and the outcomes of the clients.

Questioning insight comes from accepting ignorance and learning to ask useful and discriminating questions that test the approach to the problem.

Figure 1.1 shows one version of what is often referred to as 'Kolb's learning cycle'. The learning starts with a definite *experience*, one to which you perhaps applied programme knowledge but which is problematic when you applied it. Without a conscious learning process, that's where the 'cycle' may stop – possibly lots of action but little learning. Or, as TS Eliot (1941) put it: *We had the experience but missed the meaning, and approach to the meaning restores the experience.* If you consciously continue round the whole cycle and take time to *reflect* on the experience, ideally *sharing* your reflections with others, they can help not only by giving support but also by asking questions – questions that lead you to create your own new ideas and insights. Revans makes the point

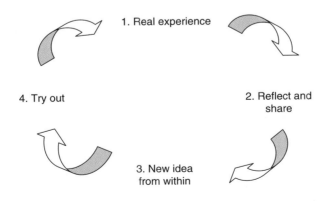

1. Real experience

2. Reflect and share

3. New idea from within

4. Try out

Figure 1.1 Experiential learning – questioning insight

that it is this new insight that brings a new perspective that in turn leads to new ideas:

> *What appears to be important is to be in at the birth of a new insight, not necessarily one's own, when there bursts forth that gasp of surprise which reveals that, at last, someone has suddenly seen a new relationship that brings new perspectives to his world.*
>
> (Revans, 1982: 603)

The generation of *new ideas* about what the experience meant and what you might do is a next step towards solving the problem. If you follow this through and take or *try out* those next steps, then you progress the problem and the cycle starts again with a new *experience* – in the process, becoming your own 'expert'.

Problems versus puzzles

Revans distinguishes between *puzzles* and *problems*. Puzzles have 'correct' solutions and can be solved via the application of programmed knowledge and with the help of experts. Traditional teaching (or *P*) supports resolving puzzles in situations in which there is a right answer, however difficult it may be to find. So, for example, you may not know the process the first time you need to recruit a new member of staff, but there is probably a procedure manual in the organisation and/or an expert (HR adviser) who can show you how. This is a puzzle, not a problem, and therefore not suitable for action learning.

Problems have no right answers and are tackled by people in different ways by the exercise of questioning insight. Action learning works with problems where there is no right answer or no one single course of action that could be taken to resolve the situation. For example, there are many books and experts to tell you how to motivate a member of staff; however, all managers will approach the problem from a different angle and depending on their own value systems, management style and past experiences.

We will see in Chapter 3 that Grint (2008) differentiates between critical, tame and wicked problems.

- Critical problems are those that demand command as a response – a person who has collapsed on the street, a child whose parents have been taken ill, a fire or flood. All of these require swift action, with little time for discussion. Many will have rehearsed responses or procedures.

- Tame problems, though they can be very demanding (such as organising the emergency team rota), are amenable to rational tools of planning and therefore are the responsibility of management. Both of these situations are in the domain of puzzles.

- Wicked problems, however, defy the rules of planning and procedure and sit in the domain of problems. They are usually messy and involve complex interdependencies, so sorting one issue out often provokes another. Tackling homelessness, eliminating poverty, working across organisational boundaries all fall into this domain. In this book, we argue that this is the domain of social work and that through action learning the social worker can resist the attempt to push wicked problems into the management domain of planning.

Four modes of learning

Before we look at how action learning and its principles fit with modes of learning, take a moment to reflect.

ACTIVITY 1.1

Think about a key learning event that influenced your practice as a social worker.

- *What happened?*
- *Where did you learn it?*
- *What was the learning process?*
- *How did you feel before, during and after the event?*
- *What did you learn?*

During a Skills for Care programme for developing action learning facilitators in 2011 and 2012, 380 social workers were asked the same questions and the responses are noted in the box below.

Where the learning occurred:

University 8%, workshop 12%, at work 42%, outside work 38%

What the learning process was:

Reading 2%, instructed and put into practice 18%, making sense of something that happened 39%, trying something new 41%

How the learning felt:

Negative 4%, positive 17%, a mix of both 79%

What was learned?

About things 12%, about doing 37%, about self 47%, about self and others 23%

How do these responses compare to your response to Activity 1.1?

The final result of the informal survey above correlates with Pedler and Aspinwall's (1995) four types of learning:

1. learning about things;

2. learning to do things;

3. learning to become yourself;

4. learning to achieve things with others.

Seven levels of learning were described through extensive research by Leary *et al.* (1986) and were subsequently combined into three by Pedler and Aspinwall (1995). These are used in combination with the four types of learning in Table 1.2.

Table 1.2 Four types and three levels of learning

Level	Type of learning			
	Learning about things	**Learning to do things**	**Learning to become yourself**	**Learning to achieve things with others**
Implementation through: Practice education Supervision	Able to recall and describe correctly facts, rules and procedures Describe established concepts and theories	Carry out existing procedures and processes correctly Follow and put into practice instructions on the correct way to do things	Accept feedback on your performance Develop with others a personal development plan that meets the gap between desired and actual performance	Recognise and respect existing norms of behaviour Understand and carry out specified roles and duties within a team
Improvement through: Supervision Action learning	Reflect on experiences and make meaning from them Think for yourself and devise own concepts, theories and hypotheses	Carry out systematic reviews to improve existing systems and processes Handle a wide variety of tasks and decide your own priorities	Actively seek, obtain and evaluate feedback on your performance and the way you manage yourself Draw up your own personal development plan and take ownership of it	Influence others by challenging norms, standards and ways of doing things when you think that these need to be improved Help colleagues, teams and their members to give excellent service to the users of the service
Innovation through: Action learning Critically reflective action learning	See overviews, large-scale patterns and interconnections Suspend judgement and critically reflect on alternative perspectives and assumptions	See differences between you and others as an asset, not a liability Work creatively with a range of 'stakeholders', and create new ways of thinking about processes and services	Understand and manage your own basic perspectives and assumptions Review and achieve your life/career objectives while doing something important for your profession, organisation, community or society	Identify a wide range of stakeholders in any situation, initiative or project Recognise and respect their feelings, positions, perspectives and world views

The first level of learning involves learning to *implement* through being taught the correct content, and how to do the right things, including rules and procedures, and being able to explain the theory that sits behind the practice. This is at the level of programmed knowledge, referred to above. Examples include being able to write a care plan for a client based on the collection of data, understanding the social work theory behind the plan (*practice education*), getting feedback on the quality of the plan and understanding the role of others in its implementation (*supervision*).

At the second level, you are learning to *improve*, learning to reflect and make your own meaning from the reflections and, through evaluating your work, make improvements. Examples include reflecting back on the experience of working with the client, evaluating the outcome against the theory and accepted practice (*supervision*), seeking ways with colleagues in the team to improve the outcomes through influencing and challenging practice (*action learning*).

At level three you are learning to *innovate* through critical reflection and through relationships with others you are able to do better things. Examples include critically reflecting in and on action in the case you are working on, considering the wider political dimension and seeking feedback on the assumptions and perspective you are taking (*critically reflective action learning*).

Components of action learning

Although there can be different approaches, action learning sets are made up of four components (Figure 1.2). They involve small groups or *sets* of people who each have a problem to tackle, and who meet in a group (often referred to as a 'set') roughly every 4–6 weeks over a period of several months. Participants (or the *person*) each talk about their *problem*, and commit to take *action* before the next meeting. Action learning focuses on individuals and how they can learn from the problem and from taking action.

1. **The person.** Usually there are six people in a set, each with an issue, problem or challenge to tackle. This is partly logistical; if there are more than six people the meeting can become rather long if each person is to present his or her issue and make progress with it. Fewer than four people would be rather light on the basic processes of support and challenge, discussed in Chapter 8. Individual members are required to show commitment to:

- taking action and reflecting on the challenge or problem;

- attending all the group/set meetings;

- supporting and challenging the other members;

- developing the group as a whole.

2. **The problem**. Each member brings his or her own issue or challenge to work on, although the issue may be one that the whole group is concerned with. It is important that:

- the issue is real for the individual and others, e.g. that it affects their work and life;
- there is no genuine right answer – that is, it cannot be solved by programmed knowledge alone;
- if there is movement on the issue the individual would feel better – that is, the individual really wants to change it.

In action learning the person (or group) is expected to tackle a real problem in the individual's practice or organisation, to implement any proposed changes and to see those through.

3. **The set**. As mentioned above, this is normally made up of about six people. Much less would be too small – not enough diversity, challenge and support; much bigger would be too large. At each meeting, as well as talking about their own problem, each member is committed to help the others by listening, supporting, asking questions, challenging and, perhaps, giving information, although advice is discouraged. Usually the set meets face to face, although increasingly with more sophisticated electronic systems, virtual action learning sets are possible.

4. **Action and learning.** Action learning involves taking action and learning from it so at each set meeting the individual critically reflects on action taken since the previous meeting with the support and challenge from set members and commits to taking action before the next one. Between the set meetings, the individual takes action on the real challenge, and so on.

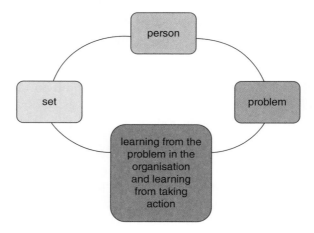

Figure 1.2 The components of action learning

How action learning is different to a discussion

Often people ask, what is the difference between what is described above and a discussion group?

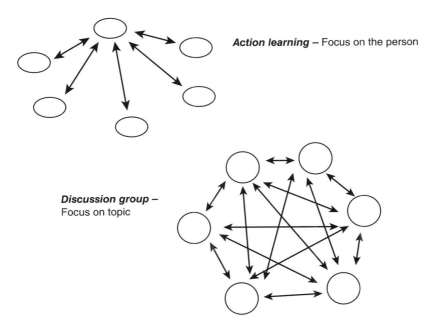

Action learning – Focus on the person

Discussion group –
Focus on topic

Figure 1.3 Modes of discussion and action learning

Pedler and Abbott (2013) offer a helpful description, with the help of Figure 1.3: *Discussion group is where the rule is to follow the topic under discussion, the action learning set keeps its focus on the person and the problem.*

PRACTICE EXAMPLE

I went to the action learning set with a problem I had implementing a particular procedure for referral to another agency. Everyone started to talk about their own problems with the procedure and it could have easily turned into a general discussion and moan about the procedure that everyone has difficulty with and we have discussed time and time again at staff meetings. But the facilitator kept focusing us back on to my problem with it. Others said that also helped them, and in me making progress on resolving the issue, others did too.

Practice education – supervision – action learning

Whilst practice education and supervision are important aspects of the management and development of the social worker, we argue that action learning provides the essential elements of critical reflection in action that are essential to the development of the profession. In Table 1.3 we summarise the relationship between action learning, practice education and supervision as complementary approaches to the development of a critically reflective practitioner.

Table 1.3 Practice education, supervision and action learning

Focus	Practice education	Supervision	Action learning
Process of learning	Driven by the curriculum Taught by subject expert Emphasis on theory Range of media used, for example, case studies, articles based on research	Mainly descriptive accounts of external training with little substance to the learning	Driven by real issues for the participants Learning with the support of peers Emphasis on learning from taking action Using each other as a resource, questioning, feedback
Size of group	Small to large groups	One to one (normally)	Closed small groups or sets
Focus of development	Group focus with participants asking questions to clarify understanding To be assessed against the curriculum or professional standards	Moving cases on to the next stage; task-oriented and prescriptive Case management Formulaic and procedural to ensure accountability	Individual in taking ownership of own problems Group in taking ownership of the process
Reflection opportunities	Usually happens after the taught session by individuals as they consider what they have learned in relation to the workplace	Limited, dependent on the supervisor–supervisee relationship, skills and time	Central to the process for both individual and group
Feedback opportunities	May be opportunities for group feedback during exercises, one-to-one feedback from the tutor/teacher in the form of assessed work	Feedback is often about procedural or meeting the organisation's expectations	Central to the process for both individual and group
Transfer of learning back to work	Can be built into assessments or done individually	Actions are built into case discussions; it is more about learning the task and process	Central to the process is taking learning back to the workplace through agreed actions
Benefits	Improved knowledge/theory	Caseload management and organisational accountability	Critical reflection skills in practice

Focus	Practice education	Supervision	Action learning
	Improvement in critical appraisal of research evidence	Opportunity for feedback	Giving and receiving feedback
		Support in a one-to-one environment	Working in a group
	Reaching a professional standard		Self-confidence
			Improvement in performance
			Presenting problems
			Questioning and listening skills
Cost	Medium	High	Low

Practice education

The literature is well represented in the role of education in social work to prepare social work students and newly qualified practitioners for the challenges of social work practice (Zlotnik, 2002; O'Connor *et al.*, 2009). Being prepared for practice includes knowledge and understanding of evidence-based practice, theory and skills – in other words, the programmed knowledge of Revans's equation.

Supervision

Supervision is described in *Providing Effective Supervision* (Skills for Care and the Children's Workforce Development Council, 2007) as *an accountable process which supports, assures and develops the knowledge, skills and values of an individual group or team*. It clearly states there are three integrated roles to supervision: (1) *line management*, including case management; (2) *professional supervision*, including reviewing and reflection on practice issues; and (3) *continuing profession development*, including constructive feedback and observation of practice. However, this vision is often not borne out in practice, with social workers reporting that the line management processes dominate supervision sessions and that the professional aspects and continuing professional development are often missing. In a study of supervision in England, South Africa and Sweden, Bradley and Hojer (2009) noted the predominance of administratively dominated supervision within management-driven social work agencies. Indeed, Noble and Irwin (2009: 352) assert that it's not just managers who are less reflective: *The new managerialism requires a new kind of worker; a worker concerned with work performance and work appraisals, work outputs and management systems.*

It could be argued that, in organisations that are risk-averse and with a society that is less tolerant of mistakes, supervision is more concerned with risk management than learning and development. Experience of action learning creating the time and space to support the professional role of supervision and developing social workers as critically reflective practitioners will be explored further in Chapter 3.

Chapter summary

- Action learning is a process of individual and professional and organisational development. Working in groups of equals, people use real, current organisational, practice and social challenges in real time to learn from their attempts to change or improve things.

- Revans founded action learning as a way of working, although never truly defined it, insisting that it is simple but cannot be communicated as a technique or method because it is ultimately concerned with a profound understanding of ourselves and the world we live in.

- There are a number of approaches that have been developed in social care. These include: (1) individuals from a wide variety of backgrounds or agencies bringing their own problems to the set; (2) action learning sets with themes, for example, all set members supporting newly qualified social workers, with each bringing his or her own issues to the action learning set; and (3) virtual synchronous and asynchronous set meetings.

- There are a number of principles involved in action learning:

  - learning must be equal to or greater than the rate of change;

  - learning is comprised of both programmed knowledge and questioning insight;

  - action learning is concerned with problems, not puzzles.

- The centrality of questions in action learning is fundamental for both theory and practice.

- Action learning has four components – the individual, the set, the problem or challenge, and the learning from taking action.

- Action learning is a complementary approach with practice education and supervision.

FURTHER READING

Pedler, M.J. and Abbott, C. (2013) *Facilitating Action Learning: A Practitioner's Guide.* London: McGraw Hill.

Revans, R.W. (2011) *ABC of Action Learning.* Farnham: Gower.

Chapter 2
Action learning and social work

PROFESSIONAL CAPABILITIES FRAMEWORK

This chapter will help you demonstrate the following capabilities:

- Professionalism 1.10 – With support, take steps to manage and promote own safety, health, wellbeing and emotional resilience.
- Knowledge 5.1 – Acknowledge the centrality of relationships for people and the key concepts of attachment, separation, loss, change and resilience.
- Contexts and Organisations 8.6 – Take responsibility for your role and impact within teams and be able to contribute positively to effective team working.
- Critical Reflection and Analysis 6.2 – With support, rigorously question and evaluate the reliability and validity of information from different sources.

Introduction

This chapter explores the relationship between social work and action learning. Social work has a requirement to perform well in areas of problem solving in real time and in real-life situations to achieve positive outcomes for service users. The performance agenda is still high on the priority list for social workers, managers and directors alike; however, it is simply not enough for statistics and other quantitative measures to realise fully the potential for social work and for other, and arguably more important, outcomes to be met with service users, carers and families. This requires a different approach to how we work, not just with service users, but also with other professional groups and in our own teams.

Action learning supports 'good practice' in social work. For example, in an action learning set, real problems and issues are raised by set members to develop thinking, understand their emotions behind the issue and take actions to bring about change. The principles of action learning fit well in social work practice; we would argue that practitioners working together *as comrades in adversity* to overcome the issues and challenges that affect their working lives is a model to aspire to (Pedler *et al.*, 2010). Moreover, the ethos of action learning is very much centred on the problem holder and others to question rather than become the experts in others' problems. This is not only helpful but fundamentally supports social workers to become 'change agents' for service users who have become disenfranchised with professionals entering their lives and telling them where they are going wrong and what to do next.

Notions of problem solving are viewed in a context of a changing shift in social work policy and practice towards outcomes-based services. However, it is also recognised that it is important for social workers to learn about the processes and relationships and for critical reflection to be at the heart of this, rather than the focus being entirely on outcomes and actions. The current situation as regards supervision is briefly analysed in this chapter as well as decision making and the 'courage and heart' to make decisions – often difficult decisions need to be made in environments when the rate of change exceeds our ability to learn (Revans, 2011; Pedler and Abbott, 2013). A brief look at our identity as social work practitioners is also explored here and further in Chapter 7.

Problem solving

Working with children, vulnerable adults, carers and families requires social work practitioners to have skills that facilitate and support problem solving. At the individual level, this might involve the use of active listening to understand the issue, supporting individuals to reflect on their actions and how they now feel. Since social work involves work with people who are often in vulnerable situations, there will be multiple instances where the skills are required in supporting real-time problem solving to affect real change. These times in a person's life are often fraught with crisis and very rarely is there a time when service users will get up in the morning and contact social care for support. It is at these crisis points when the problem-solving capacities of individuals and families have been depleted; this requires a model that is sensitive and real and has the ability genuinely to empower.

There is much literature about social workers not being the 'experts' in these situations and a move towards a partnership approach with service user inclusion in the development of social work students, learning and policy development (Tait and Lester, 2005). In the context of management education and action learning sets, Revans highlights that:

> *the undue intervention of experts carrying no personal responsibility for the real life actions . . . is, at best, ambiguous; in general opinionative; and at worst, reactionary.*

(Revans, 2011: 8)

It is clear that Revans had little time for experts in action learning sets and so was well ahead of his time when social work (and other public services) in some areas of practice continue to support external consultants to 'problem solve' in organisations and provide programmed knowledge or *P* (Chapter 1 identifies *P* in more detail). Social workers may often be viewed as experts in their fields and, whilst there is little argument that social workers can acquire a vast amount of technical knowledge and understanding, it is highly desirable also to have a workforce that gives the expert position back to the service users or the colleague who has a challenge in life. In doing so, the social worker can become a facilitator of change rather than a procurer of change. However, despite pockets of initiatives and policies that guide practitioners towards person-centred practice and the notion of the expert patient or expert service user, problem solving has become increasingly formulaic, procedural and drawn into managerialism and bureaucratism.

Thompson argues that the move away from traditional problem solving in social work can have negative consequences:

> *the traditional role of the social worker as a problem solver has tended to be de-emphasised. This shift away from the (highly skilled) problem-solving and empowering approach to a much more bureaucratic service-rationing approach (far less skilled) contributes to further deprofessionalisation.*

> (Thompson, 2012)

Thompson makes a helpful point in realising that social workers have a lot to offer in becoming facilitators of change in other people's lives, to empower and promote self-determination. It would not be helpful, for example, to complete an assessment with a service user who had recently had a bereavement with simply programmed knowledge about loss and bereavement, e.g. *a model or theory about loss*. Service users need more than this as they enter the world of emotional, social and economic change that comes with loss.

Change

The concept of problem solving needs to be seen in a context of uncertainty and change in social work. Recent austerity measures by the UK government, which have filtered down to local authorities, charities and other sectors, have resulted in rationalising resources whilst continuing with previous performance initiatives and indicators, the modernisation agenda and the idea of 'measuring outcomes'. Despite recent cuts in budgets, the mantra continues to be asserted that outcomes will still be achieved with vulnerable children and adults.

Schön (1973: 30) identifies that *institutions are characterised by 'dynamic conservatism' – a tendency to fight to remain the same*. Despite Schön's assertion, social work, which is attempting to keep up with a high rate of change, is experiencing difficulties in managing multiple changes to the profession. Revans (2011) identifies that organisations can get into trouble when the velocity of change exceeds the velocity of learning. Revans (in Boshyk and Dilworth, 2010: 7) argues that:

> *the challenge is to accelerate the rate of learning to anticipate and match the rate of change . . . when it falls out of balance, you can experience disequilibrium, disorientation, organisational run-down, or personal failure because of an inability to keep pace with the challenges being faced.*

As we have seen in Chapter 1, according to Revans's formula, learning (*L*) needs to be greater or equal to the change (*C*): $L \geq C$. Hawkins and Shohet (2012: 13) assert that this *Darwinian law of organisational survival* applies not only to the organisation but also to individuals, where *only if they are continuing to learn faster than the world they operate in is changing will they continue both to flourish at work and fulfil their potential*. There are of course professions that still promote to experts upon qualification and there are still many areas of social care practice that promote teaching of programmed knowledge (*P*) as a way of up-skilling the workforce. We would argue that there is a need for some of this taught knowledge (e.g. with law, procedures), but there is a much more urgent and important need for social work practitioners to question their insight through critically reflective practice, develop their learning about themselves and others through that process and put into action an approach which helps to solve real problems and challenges.

As social workers or social work students, you may feel you know more than the organisation does about the issues, problems and opportunities out there for service users and their carers. Your organisation may have a limited breadth of understanding of the real difficulties facing children and adults in the communities in which you practise. Serious case reviews and high-profile child deaths in the UK have often provided 'wholesale policy change' in social work practice and a review and scrutiny of managers and leaders of the responsible organisations. As Bourn and Hafford-Letchfield identify, in relation to the Climbié inquiry:

> *Laming explicitly blamed the lack of awareness, coordination and communication between politicians and senior officers within strategic partnerships for the difficult conditions faced by practitioners when working with challenging situations.*

> (Bourn and Hafford-Letchfield, 2011: 42)

In terms of social work identity, there is a lot to be done to reframe assumptions about the role we play in communities and in the organisation. A recent article in *Professional Social Work* highlighted the medical model dominance and a move to legal and medical approaches, away from psychosocial models. One social worker identified that she had experienced oppressive working conditions in a hospital, stating:

> *It was like a call centre. There was a vast volume of work and an oppressive culture. It got to the stage in that office if someone didn't cry on any given day it was an achievement . . . There was absolutely no respect for social workers . . . We couldn't articulate what our profession was and what our purpose was.*

> (BASW, 2013: 18)

In action learning, bringing individuals together to understand real problems, listen and reflect on issues and take action supports the development of a learning organisation so the sum of the parts are greater than the individual. We will explore this further in Chapter 7 when we consider the practical context of action learning, including the notion of a 'learning organisation'.

REFLECTION POINT

- *Can you think of a time currently or in the past when you have felt that the rate of external or environmental change has exceeded your ability to learn?*

- *On reflection, what were you feeling at that time (or now) and how did you react (what were your behaviours)?*

- *What do you think it might be like for service users and families who might be going through multiple changes themselves?*

- *Do you and your colleagues think you have more information/understanding than the organisation as a whole?*

Earlier in this chapter, we discussed the idea that service users often come into contact with social care when they are at points of crisis. At these times, the rate of external and internal change can go beyond the scope of service users' ability to learn and the lack of equilibrium and personal failure they might feel. Poverty, health problems, relationship difficulties and other social factors may well push the most 'rational' of human beings over the edge into a world of despair and crisis. If we believe that social workers are often involved with individuals and families in these uncertain times, then there is an opportunity for action learning to support social workers, families, service users and multi-disciplinary teams.

REFLECTION POINT

- *What do you think are the possibilities for action learning in your team or organisation?*

- *How well might it be received?*

- *Are you in an organisation that questions the norms and assumptions of current social work practice?*

Skill development

In both action learning sets and in social work, there are some key skills that are necessary to promote our abilities to *present, help others and facilitate processes.* In the 'social work world', the presenter of the problem or challenge might well be the service user or family member. Equally, it may well be the professional who is presenting the challenge to others (court, tribunals, panels, etc.). 'Helping' others is a core activity in social work and the skills required in action learning are arguably required in social work. These include listening to another person's story through active listening, giving feedback, supporting and challenging in a sensitive and an appropriate way. We will return to this in Chapter 8.

Furthermore, the facilitation of action learning sets requires very similar skills to some of the core functions in social work practice, including the chairing of meetings and coordination of assessments. Skills that require the ability to see the overall picture and time keeping as well as ensuring that each person is heard and has a voice are equally important in social work and in action learning sets. We will return to this in Chapters 8 and 9. Some of skills transferable between action learning sets and social work practice are identified below (Pedler, 2008; Revans, 2011; Pedler and Abbott, 2013):

- presenting a problem (analysing and describing a situation accurately);
- receiving feedback, giving feedback;
- promoting decision making;
- emotional intelligence (self-belief, empathy, understanding);
- active listening skills;
- challenging and supporting others in adversity;
- developing the ability to ask good questions.

Decision making

Decision making is a core social work activity, whether it is about key decisions relating to the welfare of a child or whether it is about a decision that is needed to safeguard a vulnerable adult. There is no clear-cut, singular method to making a decision and, despite a number of models purporting to support decision-making processes, it is still a grey area that involves cognition and, importantly, emotions that result in action. Concepts of risk management and 'best interests' can be found widely in social work literature, law and policy, although little attention is given to the validity and reliability of these approaches. Cognitive linear tests which support decision making are often used to establish a course of action, although there is a dearth of integration and acknowledgement of emotion in such 'tests' and assessments (Brown, 2011).

An example of this for social workers in adult services is the Mental Capacity Act. Social workers and health professionals are required by law to undertake such assessments as necessary to determine whether someone has capacity or not regarding a specific decision which is time-specific. Critically, this involves, amongst others, whether someone can weigh up a decision and retain that decision for long enough to make that decision. The focus therefore is linear and does not highlight the emotions behind the decision making. For example, what does the person feel when you discuss the idea of moving into residential care? Can these feelings be described? Removing emotions and believing that, as social workers, we can remain objective, rational and cognitive is at best a fallacy and at worst, dangerous. How we feel as humans impacts on our motivations, beliefs and our thinking patterns which in turn will determine a course of action (Howe, 2008).

Morrison helpfully argues:

> *Emotions play a central role in decision making. The illusion that they can be somehow removed or put on ice whilst rational decision making is in progress is neither helpful nor possible. Equally, the failure to manage feelings compromises the balance between thought, feeling and action.*

> (Morrison, 2007: 12)

In Chapter 8 you will become aware of the importance of asking questions to uncover the thinking, feeling and willing aspects of the issue. Helping the presenter of the problem with the complex exploration of emotion is not an easy task and may require the presenter to take a leap of faith to expose and describe his or her feelings. This can be tricky if the culture of the organisation or team is one that diminishes the importance of even stating how one feels. How often is it that we ask how someone is and expect a neat reply of 'fine, thank you' without the true understanding of how another person is truly feeling? It might be too difficult to undertake such a task in a team of 20 but it is certainly possible to start becoming aware of your own emotions and those of others in small action learning sets. Arguably, in doing so, as social workers we can become astute to what really makes us feel a certain way and genuinely explore our values and beliefs in a supportive environment. Revans was committed to helping others and, as Pedler (2012: 13) notes, *in contrast to more cognitive and individualistic learning theories, heart and courage are as important as intelligence and insight in action learning.* The ideas of social and emotional intelligence will be developed further in Chapter 4.

REFLECTION POINT

- *How well do you express your emotions?*
- *Does your team or organisation readily allow for such expression?*
- *What are the benefits to understanding the emotions of ourselves and others when it comes to making decisions?*
- *Do you find it easier or more difficult to make decisions in groups? Why?*

Reflective practice

Reflection is something I do all the time was the last thing we heard when speaking to a colleague about reflective practice. Although the statement appeared to be a little grandiose, it at least helped us to reflect on what we really mean when it comes to such an important task in social work and in learning. Donald Schön's contributions in *The Reflective Practitioner* and specifically on reflection 'in action' and 'on action' direct the reader away from 'technical-rationality' (a positivist epistemology of practice) and instead towards professionals using their 'artistry in doing':

> *The practitioner allows himself to experience surprise, puzzlement, or confusion in a situation which he finds uncertain or unique. He reflects on the phenomenon before him, and on the prior understandings which have been implicit in his behaviour. He carries out an experiment which serves to generate both a new understanding of the phenomenon and a change in the situation.*

(Schön, 1983: 68)

In action learning, reflection is a key component to learning where new understanding of a situation occurs through questions that help this 'puzzlement' and 'confusion'. Schön would describe this as reflection 'on action' rather than reflection 'in action' (which is more about thinking on one's feet). There is often limited scope in social work supervision to reflect on action, despite models and policy directed toward such concepts. Arguably, this is largely due to organisational cultures that are risk-adverse; this approach permeates down to social work practitioners on the ground and their supervisors. As a result of this fear and reactionary culture, much time is spent on writing up every possible case note and forgetting some of the most important areas of social work practice. Important areas include reflection and understanding our emotional responses to service users, situations and crises, to name a few.

Hawkins and Shohet (2012: 18) identify five levels of reflection which are relevant to action learning:

1. *Noticing the phenomena* – using our senses to hear and feel, without making judgements or interpretations;

2. *Recognising the patterns that connect different aspects of the phenomena* – this requires us to move from phenomena and data, not to judgement but to seeing the patterns that join the dots of the various phenomena;

3. *Making sense of the patterns* – only when we have started to see connecting patterns is it sensible to try and understand what is emerging;

4. *Shifting the frame of our perception* – this is a shift from viewing an experience in a current framework which is widely accepted or seen as 'normal' and 'how things are done around here' to critical reflection and transformational learning;

5. *Shifting one's underlying belief system* – a deeper level of reflection where a reflection on perspective occurs. Motivation and belief systems, which are often out of conscious awareness, are reflected upon.

Reflecting on our belief systems, the phenomena around us and our motivations is helpful in shifting our perceptions and is critical to the learning cycle. Without reflection there is no learning as there is no perceptual shift that can create new ways of thinking and new actions ready to be tested out. We argue throughout this book that it is not enough simply to describe your experiences, although this may well be the starting point; it is important to dig beneath the skin of the problem and to develop critically reflective practice. We will explore this in more depth in the next chapter.

ACTIVITY **2.1**

In the middle of a piece of paper, write the words 'Reflective practice' and from that centre, write what reflective practice means to you.

You could write what you think reflective practice means, how you feel about it in practice (if you do it at all) and what you can do to improve your and your organisation's reflective skills.

Finally, take your ideas into supervision as an agenda item and have a discussion with your supervisor about your thoughts and feelings.

In a learning journal, you can now reflect on that process – was anything different from your original assumptions? How did it feel? What, if anything, are you going to do in supervision differently next time?

Supervision

Critically, current models of social work supervision in local authorities and third-sector organisations typically take place between someone with implied 'super vision' and a supervisee. The relationship is often expert-led and a high percentage of time is spent working through cases with the aim of ensuring that social workers are making 'good decisions' and not putting service users (or the organisation) at risk. Often, there is little time spent on how the supervisee feels and reflective practice is something that is talked about, but not really enacted in practice.

Much literature has focused on what good supervision looks like and there are several models on offer for supervisors and supervisees to follow (Stoltenberg and Delworth, 1987; Bernard and Goodyear, 1992; Kadushin, 1992). Generally, far less attention is paid to developing group supervision or group work to support social workers with casework, problem solving and decision making. Despite the lack of popularity of group supervision, Hawkins and Shohet (2012: 178) suggest there are some advantages to such a model:

- Supervisors can see more supervisees by conducting supervision groups.

- The group can provide a supportive atmosphere of peers, sharing anxieties and realising that others are facing similar issues.

- Supervisees receive reflections, feedback, sharing and inputs from colleagues and the group supervisor.

- The group provides a way for the supervisor to test out their emotional or intuitive response to the material presented.

- The group provides a wide range of life experience and there is more likelihood of someone within the group being able to empathise with the supervisee and the client.

- Groups provide more opportunity to use action techniques.

- Group supervision, where possible, should reflect the work context which is being supervised.

Revans would probably argue strongly that a group supervision model looks quite different from an action learning set model. There are no 'experts' in action learning: the problem holder is the expert in his or her own problem and no one else. Revans also questioned the ongoing involvement of the facilitator claiming that the facilitator would only *launch the set quickly into its discussions, there may be a need when it is first formed for some supernumerary* (Revans, 2011: 9). Moreover, supervision often deals with 'puzzles' rather than 'wicked problems', as described by Grint (2005), which are *messy, circular and aggressive*. Wicked problems cannot be solved by rational analysis and solutions ready to hand from the rational supervisor or manager. Instead, there is a requirement for collaboration and action learning for such challenges where there is no 'right' or 'wrong' answer.

Boshyk and Dilworth (2010: 26) note that if there is 'magic' in action learning, the key ingredients that Revans expressed are:

- *Asking fresh questions* – this becomes a natural occurrence when people are separated from what they know.

- *Unfreezing underlying assumptions* – since few old assumptions seem applicable when you are on unfamiliar ground, the person turns to fresh questions and, from these, discovers that some of the assumptions long held to be true do not hold up well under examination.

- *Creating new connections and mental models* – this becomes possible when you move beyond the constraints imposed by assumptions and ways of thinking that are not relevant to the task at hand.

- *Rebalancing P and Q* – one outcome of the process is a new framework for *P* that is held to be valid. Some *P* is jettisoned, other *P* is created, and some *P* is either modified or validated. What drives this are the new forms of questions that emerge, and they evolve as the action learning progresses.

Critically, the rebalancing of *P* and *Q* for a number of organisations that still rely heavily on external consultants and 'experts' is a difficult prospect. It is also challenging for supervisors and managers who are in a hierarchical system that assumes that, because an individual is on a higher pay grade, that individual must have superior knowledge which others do not. It is possible that the person's understanding of puzzles might be enhanced but what of the skills required in supervision to question and unfreeze old assumptions? In this case the skill set required is different from that of the manager or supervisor who is knowledgeable about the Children Act or Mental Health Act (*P*). Supervisors and supervisees clearly need to have some grounding in policy, law and other areas but, alone, this is not enough to develop transformational learning at a deeper level and become critically conscious and critically reflective in practice (Mezirow, 1991).

ACTIVITY 2.2

Write down ten words that describe your current experience of supervision.

- *Reflecting on your last supervision, what did you find helpful? Did you genuinely feel that you became 'unstuck' from your problems/challenges?*

- *What do you think are the key differences between supervision and action learning?*

- *What sort of problems are best supported in supervision/group supervision and what are best supported in action learning sets?*

- *Do you have any assumptions about supervision?*

Action learning is not just about sitting down with your social care colleagues in a room and attempting to get down to some action and learning. It is a methodology which can be used widely in social work practice to support the solving of 'wicked problems' as they arise. From supervision to working with complex family situations, it helps the practitioner, the service user and others involved to reframe their perspective on the issue or challenge at hand. By reflecting on their previous actions, feelings and thoughts it is possible to think about a situation with 'a new lens'. Helping others to see things (and feel things) in a new light is a powerful tool for social workers to have. In supervision, you will at times need to reflect on what you have managed to achieve with a service user, family or carer, although you may become 'stuck' at some point. Having a supervisor to ask fresh questions, support your reflections and get down to some action will help your learning *about* the situation in a new light and also support your awareness about how *you* learn.

CASE STUDY **2.1**

NQSW action learning set across adult social work teams

A small group of newly qualified social workers (NQSWs) set up an action learning set across several adult social care teams with the help of a facilitator who was a senior practitioner in one of the teams. Their first meeting was full of enthusiasm and commitment to support each other in real problem solving. Ground rules were established and the facilitator supported the programmed knowledge (P) that was required for each NQSW to understand the steps in the process. Time keeping was essential for each of the participants to have time to explore their issue in enough depth whilst balancing this with everyone else getting a chance to work through their challenge. Some of the challenges raised were specifically related to the relationship they had with a family member or service user which created a feeling of being 'stuck'. Other issues related to the challenges of working with a particular colleague in their team or externally, e.g. with a health professional/team. The issues raised had no 'rational' answer and all of the learning set members were able to challenge, probe and ask fresh questions, which helped the problem holder to see the problem through a new lens. After a year, an evaluation form was sent to each member of the group to get a sense of their views on action learning:

> I was able to develop my skills at reflecting on my experience by asking questions about my feelings, thoughts, behaviours and I also applied these questioning techniques when appropriate with my colleagues and service users.
>
> *(Social worker)*

> It [action learning] allows for deeper exploration of work complexities allowing to generate more ideas and to choose one's attitude to the work. It is beneficial to be able to share with other practitioners and also to be able to support them in their exploration.
>
> *(Social work manager)*

> The sets have helped me to reflect on how I think about issues, why I think that way, how I feel and to think of alternative solutions.
>
> *(Social work team leader)*

> I will always endeavour to find time and space to reflect on how I am performing as this has proved to be beneficial in my practice. I have found it refreshes my mind and the way I react to situations.
>
> *(Social worker)*

Chapter summary

- Social work involves working with complex and challenging issues in real time, often in situations of crisis where rational, cognitive decision-making models are ineffective.

- Action learning sets can support decision making, with the focus on the problem holder being the 'expert' in the situation rather than a facilitator; the latter is seen as ambiguous and unhelpful.

- Change is constant (particularly in social work and social care) and Revans's formula highlights the need for learning to keep up with the velocity of external change.

- A number of skills developed in learning sets can be utilised in the social work task, including assessment, care planning, investigations and capacity 'tests'.

- Current methods of supervision can be 'expert-led', both in individual and group settings. Action learning supports practitioners to reflect and reframe and facilitates an emotional shift to develop new action and learning.

- Action learning in social work is not always going to work, particularly for puzzles where 'the answer is out there'. It is however a methodology that can support decision making for messy, complex 'wicked problems' which are plentiful in the situations in which social workers find themselves.

- Action learning is often supported by organisations which are 'learning organisations' and open to challenge normative assumptions relating to social work policy, principles and practice.

FURTHER READING

Hawkins, P. and Shohet, R. (2012) *Supervision in the Helping Professions,* 4th edn. Berkshire: Open University Press.

Morrison, T. (2007) Emotional intelligence, emotion and social work: context, characteristics, complications and contribution. *British Journal of Social Work,* 37 (2): 245–263.

Revans, R. (2011) *ABC of Action Learning.* Farnham: Gower Publishing.

Chapter 3

Action learning and critically reflective practice

Introduction

This chapter introduces the idea of critically reflective practice within action learning. It argues that there is a need to question assumptions about what is prescribed as 'good practice' and the evidence base which underpins assessment and interventions with service users/carers. The action learning methodology is highlighted as helpful in supporting social workers to reflect critically on their practice within a wider social and professional context. It considers the notion of the social worker as a tempered radical championing emancipation for service users and the profession. As The College of Social Work (2012) highlights, *critical reflection entails insight, exploratory and creative thinking for each unique piece of practice* and, importantly, *over time, social work practitioners should become highly skilled in this*.

Critical reflection and critically reflective practice are central to social work. 'Critical reflection and analysis' is a central feature of The College of Social Work's Professional Capabilities Framework (PCF), and is required to different degrees in all levels of social work practice. The PCF expects the integration of critical reflection into all social work practice, and the ability to apply critical reflective skills is a key aspect of social worker development.

> *Critical reflection and critically reflective practice are central to social work – indeed 'Critical Reflection and Analysis' is one of the nine domains of the PCF, with capability statements built into all levels.*

(The College of Social Work, 2012)

The linking of critical reflection and action learning started to appear in the 1990s when academics in business schools began to challenge the rational and technical approach to professional development, and specifically management development. Action learning, as we have seen in Chapter 1, offers a different approach by focusing on learning from peers and from real-life problems and challenges in practice. However, linking critical reflection and drawing on critical social theory, we start to consider how action and learning are constrained and shaped by politics and power in human systems (Trehan and Pedler, 2010). So in the context of social work social workers are encouraged to remove themselves from the organisational and cultural domain they work in and ask more fundamental questions of their practice:

> *Critical action learning goes beyond 'ordinary criticality' to question existing practices, structures and power relations within the organisation. It does this by encouraging the practices of critical thinking and reflection, and distinguishes between effective practice, reflective practice and critically reflective practice.*

(Pedler and Abbott, 2013: 120)

Critical reflection in action learning

In action learning, we have seen in Chapter 1 that Revans distinguishes between puzzles where there is a tested and prescribed solution, and problems where *no single course of action is to be justified . . . so that different managers, all reasonable, experienced and sober, might set out by treating them in markedly different ways* (Revans, 2011: 6–10).

Revans's description of a problem is similar to that of Rittel and Webber (1973) and Grint (2008) who develop the idea of 'wicked problems'. In his leadership model (Figure 3.1), Grint proposes a threefold typology of problems where the progression from 'critical' to 'tame' to 'wicked' shows up in increased uncertainty about solutions and with a much greater need for collaboration (Grint, 2008: 11–18).

Problems such as a heart attack, leaving a homeless person on the street in sub-zero conditions, the flooding of a housing estate or a fire in an office block are often dealt with by the blue light or emergency services. Such problems are critical in that they demand swift action, leaving little time for discussion or

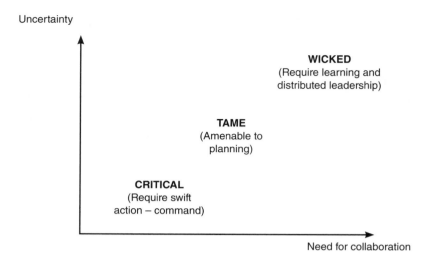

Figure 3.1 Three types of problem (from Pedler and Abbott, 2013: 19)

uncertainty. 'Tame' problems, such as planning heart surgery or building flood defences, can be very complicated, but tame because they respond to the tools of rational planning and management. The wicked problems defy rational analysis and planning and are characterised by a high degree of uncertainty. They are often messy, involving new ways of working, and require the collaboration of a number of people or organisations; for example, eliminating homelessness or child poverty in a neighbourhood, motivating people or working in multi-agency settings are all examples of problems which are complex and unpredictable in this way. Any one solution proposed is likely to generate other problems; there are no right or wrong answers, but only better or worse alternatives. Working with wicked problems requires distributed leadership, a high degree of collaboration and a great deal of learning.

Organisations such as local authorities that are primarily designed to work with tame problems, i.e. those that require planning, albeit sophisticated planning, are at odds with the wicked problems of social work, i.e. that are both uncertain and complex and require collaboration between agencies and users of services. Social workers are likely to be faced with situations that fit the description of wicked in the course of their work. The College of Social Work's PCF (2012) does not use the language of wicked issues or problems, but defines professional capability as including the ability to *apply the principles of critical thinking, reasoned discernment [and] critical reflection and analysis to increasingly complex cases* and *provide critical reflection, challenge and evidence-informed decision-making in complex situations*.

Social workers are expected not only to master these demanding analytical skills, but also to act on their judgements. According to the PCF, an experienced social worker should be able to *manage potentially conflicting or competing values and ethical dilemmas to arrive at principled decisions*, and even to pursue such issues in wider forums: *Raise and address issues of poor practice, internally through the organisation, and then independently if required* (The College of Social Work, 2012).

The data collected in a small research study (Pedler *et al.*, 2013) revealed the social worker to be more centred on self and personal practices than on the 'wicked issues' of social work and society. The report suggests that these findings could indicate an inner concern with self and personal practice as a defence against anxiety, as defined by Menzies Lyth (1960) in nursing staff in hospitals. The conditions of social work are comparable to those in the health service where *Hospitals are institutions cradled in anxiety* and where everyone, from patients to junior staff to senior clinicians and managers, is anxious and subject to crises (Revans, 1982: 263). The study went on to look at when critical action learning supported the social worker in taking this more critical look at his or her practice.

CASE STUDY 3.1

My problem was a case I had that involved a young man with learning disabilities who had lived in residential care since he was six years old. He had severe communication problems and it was assumed that he would transfer to an adult residential care facility. There were some complex family issues as well and my problem was which facility was going to be the best.

The set helped me look at the problem with fresh eyes – this young man had been on my caseload for only a very short time and I was challenged about the reports I was given by the residential care home. These questions were very helpful from a technical point of view, but then one person asked about my role as the care manager/broker and I started to get quite upset. I remember saying, 'I am a social worker, not a broker'. The questioner asked me gently what was the difference and what value could a social worker offer over care management?

I remember not being very coherent in my answer – it was quite a shock and I asked for time to reflect on the implications that threw up for me. The set suggested that we return to my issue at the end of the day, which I was really grateful for.

When the set returned to my issue I asked if I could change the issue to ask to help me rediscover my social work head and heart in this issue. I was a bit nervous about this as my manager was in the set and it felt like I was exposing my underbelly.

The group started to help me explore the problem using the core values of social work and I soon realised that the management processes I had been asked to follow were preventing me from serving this person in the way he deserved. Or, more to the point, I was allowing the care planning approach to prevent me from doing what I should be doing as a social worker. It was a revealing moment for me. Why was I doing that – fear, inability to challenge, wanting to be a part

---

---

of the team and fit in? Did other people feel as I did? What was I doing having this conversation in front of my managers?

The facilitator asked me to put all the organisational politics to one side, all the resource issues, etc. and just paint a picture of what a social worker response to the case would be. I wasn't sure but suggested that for the next meeting I would try. It was really liberating to be free of the other stuff and I found as I started to talk that I could. At the next meeting, I fed back my picture and the group helped me explore what I could take that was realistic to support this young man. The manager was actually very helpful here.

The end result . . . Well, this was 18 months ago. X is now living in a sheltered housing complex, and having discovered a joy and ability to do kitchen work is at college one day a week doing catering. Although at the moment he works two days a week on the complex, there are plans for him to get a job in the village pub kitchen.

It's been hard work but the results are great and much better than X just being a case transfer from one facility to another.

(Case study from Pedler et al., 2013)

- *Describe a situation when you had a 'wicked' problem.*
- *How did you respond?*
- *What does your response say about you as a social worker?*
- *How did you manage the situation?*
- *What emotions were involved for you?*

Revans suggested that action learning was designed precisely for these problematic situations. The purpose of the action learning set is to help people to face up to the difficult issues and not to avoid them. The peer support and challenge of the set are designed to encourage colleagues to tackle problems in practice through experimentation, action and learning. In the case above, without such support and challenge, it was likely that a critical perspective on the case would have been lost and the impact therefore on the service user would have been less positive. In her study of nursing, Menzies Lyth (1960) points out how risky situations can result in the strengthening of rigid rules and hierarchies as a *defence against anxiety*. Here in this case the care management approach reduced the risk, but at what cost? By allowing the social worker time and space to explore the case from a wider professional perspective she was able to address care management in a different way.

> *What is . . . abundantly clear is that there is a desire amongst social workers, service users, directors and managers for the profession to be liberated from the care management strait-jacket so as to be able to be creative and focused on problem-solving in its approach to supporting users and carers.*

(The College of Social Work, 2012)

Revans (1971) recognised that organisational culture and politics play an important part in the learning process. Indeed, as we will see in Chapter 9, he insisted that the primary role of the facilitator is to ensure the right conditions are created and nurtured. Brookfield (1987: 12) makes the point that critical thinking *is not seen as a wholly rational mechanical activity. Emotive aspects – feelings, emotional responses, intuitions, sensing – are central to critical thinking in adult life.* We return to this in Chapter 4.

Willmott (1994, 1997) arguably started the debate about critical action learning, arguing that conventional action learning, when those in the set share a dominant ideology and set of values, means that they will not question their practices from a critical perspective. Raelin (2008: 523) joined this debate, arguing that those of the same profession are socialised into practices and values via what he describes as *cultural doping*.

In the case we looked at above:

- Would a team meeting or supervision session lead to the same results?

- Would the social worker's learning be captured by the organisation and care management processes?

- Would any fundamental change have happened for the social worker, the organisation or the service user?

If not, then supervision or a case review process may be employed to do harm, not good by being controlled by the powerful.

The idea is that, through critical reflection in action learning, the set member, with the support of peers, *emancipates* professional learning from the technical, functional or 'management by numbers' preoccupations of the organisation. It attempts to do this by promoting an understanding of how learning and action in teams, organisations, multi-agency settings, professional networks and societies are structured and governed by power and politics. *Action learning can encourage an awareness of the primacy of politics, both macro and micro, and the influence of power on decision making and non-decision making, not to mention the 'mobilisation of bias'* (McLoughlin and Thorpe, 1993: 25).

Action learning involves engaging with these political, emotional and cultural processes to deal with the problems in the swampy lowlands of practice, and in doing so, to reduce oppression and broaden the boundaries of freedom. Often these problems are difficult because they are constantly changing, the meaning for each of the stakeholders is different, and resolving one aspect of the problem reveals another or plain common sense is not so commonly used. Critical reflection in action learning offers a different approach and aims to reveal issues that are often disguised or avoided. In the process, it can, as we have seen from the case study, be *really liberating,* freeing us from established ways of doing things into new ways of working.

Critical reflection

Critically reflective practice, as we have seen, is a core aspect of a social worker's formation and professional development. The College of Social Work's PCF makes it plain that this is something expected even in any student's practice, and then, in increasing depth and complexity, throughout the social worker's professional development and career progression. The ability to reflect, and thereby to correct or vary one's reactions to the situation, becomes an affirmation of being a professional social worker. Indeed, Schön's (1983) notion of what it is to be a professional is the ability to reflect 'in action' and 'on action'.

The concept of reflection varies from the private thought, for example, a journal or diary without an action, considering some information before action, usually in a learning environment, for example, in experiential learning (Dewey, 1933), to the mental process of making sense of an issue for which there is not an apparent answer (King and Kitchener, 1994). Schön (1983) describes the process of reflecting in action, drawing on ingrained, 'tacit' knowledge to make spontaneous decisions about events as they happen, and reflecting on action, the reflection that takes place when contemplating an action or after an action is taken. Killon and Todnew (1991) draw together reflection in action and on action as the practitioner makes decisions about future action on the basis of what happened during a particular event and the reflection that occurred afterwards. Stoll *et al.* (2003) say that another kind of reflection is meta-learning – learning about your own learning.

Reed and Proctor (1993) describe *critical* reflection as the process of looking back critically at one's own action and combining this with the technical and ethical aspects of professional knowledge to tackle new situations. They emphasise that in this process there is implicit a widening range of considerations other than the original event. All these writers focus on the reflective process being an individual one and designed to improve individual performance; this would appear to complement the finding of the small-scale research project described above which proposes that the social worker is centred on self and personal practices. However, Reynolds (1998) distinguishes critical reflection from other forms of reflection as being more concerned with questioning assumptions, a social rather than individual focus, the analysis of power relations and emancipation. These ideas of liberation and emancipation are drawn from the work of Habermas (1979), who distinguished emancipatory learning as one of three domains of learning. In this context, learning concerns social workers becoming aware of the forces that have brought them or their case to the current situation and taking action to change the situation. As Apps noted:

> *Emancipatory learning is that which frees people from personal, institutional, or environmental forces that prevent them from seeing new directions, from gaining control of their lives, their society and their world.*

> (Apps, 1985: 151)

This use of critical reflection in a collective and public environment, that is, the action learning set, to make sense of complex and ambiguous problems which are of great relevance for organisational development and learning has gained importance in the literature (Vince, 2002; Nicolini *et al.*, 2004; Reynolds and Vince, 2004a, b). Trehan argues that critical action learning supports this effort to:

> *create new understandings by making conscious the social, political, professional, economic and ethical assumptions constraining or supporting individual and collective action in a specific context.*

> (Trehan, 2011: 187)

Critical reflection in action learning therefore positions itself as a vehicle that promotes a deepening of critical thinking by emphasising the value of collective and also more public (Raelin, 2001) reflection as well as individual reflection on professional life.

CASE STUDY 3.2

The case I brought to my set was about the introduction of hot-desking in the authority. My team had been office-based in a small community building and now under an accommodation review was being told that the offices would be closed and staff would be hot-desking in the main city offices. This was causing all sorts of problems for the staff. Mainly to do with car parking; at the time we had free car parking – the thought of paying £10 a day to park didn't go down well. There were also the issues of childcare; many staff lived locally and going in and out of the city was going to lengthen the working day. As part of the management team I was seen as the person to blame.

The set was made up of a number of different local authorities, including managers from the city centre base we would be working with in the new scheme. They were all very sympathetic to the problem and I felt I got a lot of emotional support from them. I know I was there to resolve the issue but actually, I felt so alone in the day job that I just needed people to listen – really listen without jumping down my throat – as my team did. At the third meeting one of the set suggested that I was displaying helpless victim behaviour, which hit me. She was right of course and it did get me thinking about what this was doing to me and whether I was allowing the team to see me this way too. Another of the set presented his problem and I was open-mouthed with astonishment. He was the manager of the city-based team that we would be joining; his issue was his staff being annoyed about the outlying community-based teams hot-desking with them! They felt the community teams were spoilt with no car parking fees, shorter working days without the commute; they wondered whether the rumours were true that there would be compensation given to these staff and the unfairness of this. Then another from learning and development talked about the problem of supporting newly qualified staff in a hot-desking environment where teams rarely meet face to face. I remember asking why these problems had aired themselves now, and they said they had been talking about them since the first set meeting, hadn't I been listening? Well no, I hadn't, clearly. I had been so involved in my own issue and using the group as a listening forum I hadn't heard my colleagues' problems. This was a real revelation to me. Was I listening to anybody? Had I imagined this problem? I, too, was nervous about the move; was I using others' views to give my own validity? The three of us made the decision to agree some data collection questions for the teams regarding the move; one said she would look at any research about hot-desking environments. I agreed to spend the day in the city centre base with the other manager and vice versa.

At the next meeting we presented back the data we had collected and asked the others to interrogate it on the three levels we had been shown how to use: thinking, feeling and willing. It was fascinating listening to the conversations that followed; the group suggested that we sit outside the circle and just listen.

There was no evidence from a rational/technical point of view as to why this would not work; the planners were right, dare I say. The real problem was there was no way the organisation was allowing the feelings of people to be taken into account so therefore everyone was trying to find technical/rational arguments to justify feelings that were not allowed in the system. And that was stopping everyone moving forward. Staff continuing to find any technical reason why it wouldn't work and senior management getting more exasperated. So what would happen if we met with our managers and said just that? What if the real problem was feelings needed to be acknowledged and addressed? How would an organisation so immersed in planning and project change view this?

Well, we did. It took a lot of perseverance. At first we thought the managers just saw this as 'great, that's sorted, then, everyone accepts the move so let's move on'.

We kept taking the issue back to the set, we tried other approaches, and we did get through in the end. The communication team was commissioned by the senior managers to get the message across that they were listening but we suggested this wasn't appropriate: what staff needed was authentic 'them speaking'. And they did. We also suggested that both teams move, albeit that one would only be moving in the building. This would feel like a new team starting rather than one 'moving over' to accommodate another. Both teams have been involved in landing the new space. We did suggest that the senior managers set up an action learning set as well.

The moves happen in April . . . There are certainly less objections and we have planned the community team end of building party and the city team has as well and then a new office opening. Hold this space . . .

(Reproduced from Pedler et al., 2013)

In the case above individuals were encouraged to share their reflections on a particular situation, interrogate them and push them further. They started to recognise what Vince (2002) terms *organizing insight*, that is, the role politics plays in the learning process. In this case, Revans's saying, *Sets for reflection; projects for action* was acted out. The set helped individuals to add to their own experiences of action (learning from experience) via a collective reflection in the set on the organisational dynamics created in action (learning from organising).

ACTIVITY **3.1**

Consider a recent case you have been involved in and discuss the following in your team or set.

- *What do my practices say about my assumptions and beliefs?*
- *How did my assumptions guide my actions?*
- *What views of power do they embody?*
- *Whose interests are being served by my practices?*
- *What is it that constrains my views about what is possible?*

(Adapted from Smyth, 1989)

Below is an activity you could try within a team as a way of introducing critical reflection.

Alternative stances

This activity can be done via email between the members of an action learning set. It works better in a virtual rather than a face-to-face (f2f) setting because it gives each person some time to think and perhaps to read up on his or her stance.

Choose a problem situation from one of the members that seems especially complex or confusing. Perhaps a set member has been put in a complicated or 'political' situation or perhaps a member is faced with a seemingly impossible dilemma.

1. The person concerned with the difficult situation first emails his or her colleagues with a brief description of the situation.

At the foot of this description the situation owner should add the following stances:

- *Marxist;*
- *Feminist;*
- *Environmentalist;*
- *Free market economist;*
- *NIMBY (not in my back yard);*
- *Anti-colonial campaigner.*

And then the situation owner allocates each set member to a different stance.

2. Each member then responds to the email from the allocated stance within an agreed time frame, say within one week, or in time for the next meeting.

N.B.: Members can do any research they wish to work out their stance and the likely position to be taken on the issue. The aim is to work from the value position of that stance to propose an analysis and give suggestions for action.

3. When all the stances have been posted, the person who initiated the exchange should then summarise the insights gained from the process together with any new questions.

4. If possible, an f2f meeting is probably best suited to digesting the outcomes of this activity and especially with helping the person with the next steps.

(From Pedler and Abbott, 2013)

Social workers as tempered radicals

In 2011 The College of Social Work organised a series of summits to explore the role of the social worker in adult social care. One of the themes that emerged was that of a profession whose core values and identity were often at odds with the dominant organisational culture and practices they operated in. Example statements included, 'our role is to challenge on behalf of vulnerable adults', 'not taking the most organisationally convenient answer', 'we have to challenge the status quo' and 'we must not be afraid of irritating the system when its needed'.

Throughout this book we propose that social workers need more than training and education (or programmed knowledge) in order to challenge the status quo and stand up against inequalities and injustices on behalf of our society. Action learning and, indeed, critically reflective action learning support social workers through the challenges and opportunities that this brings.

Attwood (2007) proposed the action learner and we propose a social worker as a tempered radical – a notion described originally by Meyerson (2003) as people who identify with and are committed to their organisations, but who are simultaneously committed to a set of core values and identity in decision making which differs fundamentally from the dominant culture of their organisations. They are:

> *people who want to succeed in their organisations yet want to live by their values or identities, even if they are somehow at odds with the dominant culture of their organisations . . .*
>
> *Tempered radicals want to fit in and they want to retain what makes them different. They want to rock the boat, and they want to stay in it.*
>
> (Meyerson, 2003: xi)

The tempered radical therefore is a position standing both in and outside the organisation as the basis for judgements and actions. In terms of The College of Social Work summits, this translates into a strong professional identity, in that when members of a profession act in ways that outwardly express their stated values, they make that part of themselves real. The essential part of living by and through the core values is emphasised by Meyerson (2003: 89) as *when it comes time to evaluate a course of action – what to do – how far to push – what to give up.*

Adams and Balfour (2004) introduce us to the notion of *administrative evil.* By that they mean the culture of technical rationality enabling a form of evil that is masked. That is, when people can engage in acts of evil without being aware that they are in fact doing anything at all wrong. So social workers may simply be acting according to their organisational role, meeting the demands of the job description, meeting the targets set and getting good performance reviews and yet being active participants in what could be described as administrative evil, usually well after the event! Even worse, according to Adams and Balfour (2004: 4), under conditions of what they call *moral inversion,* in which:

> *something evil has been redefined convincingly as good, ordinary people can too easily engage in acts of administrative evil while believing that what they are doing is not only correct, but in fact good.*

The concept of professional identity has engaged social workers over recent years (Payne, 2006). Expert knowledge and the application of technical rationality are arguably the lifeblood of a profession and over the last 15 years there has been evidence of social work responding to this by the drive for academic qualifications, from Certificate level to postgraduate qualifications. This recognised specialised knowledge gives power, control and legitimacy to act. However, the compartmentalisation of knowledge can lead to a context-free practice, one that is dominated by compliance, where the social worker's practice is providing legal responses to cases. Guerreiro-Ramos in Adams and Balfour (2004) argues that this practice of a profession with no sense of context prevents a meaningful engagement with the larger ethical and political concerns of society. So responsibility for the prevention of acts of administrative evil rests, in part, with social workers who are tempered radicals and understand their role and professional identity in such a way that they highlight the temptations that exist within *moral inversions*.

Being a tempered radical and critical thinker, as we have seen from the accounts above, can be very liberating and transform the way we work in practice. However there is a dark side and Meyerson (2003: 38) advises that practitioners need to *armour themselves against the battle of hostility*. Brookfield (1987: 11) recognised that developing critical thinking in others is problematic: *we can however try to awaken, prompt, nurture and encourage this process without making people feel threatened or patronised.* When those skills have been developed and are being utilised, Brookfield's (1994) research showed that people often suffered from the following:

- feelings of 'impostorship' – doubting one's worthiness to question the organisation or profession;

- 'lost innocence' – from self-questioning of one's own personal taken-for-granted ideas;

- despair at the implications of taking a radical analysis of their professional context;

- 'cultural suicide', in encountering other people's hostility at their critical questioning of accepted practices.

It is for these reasons that Revans referred to action learning set members as *comrades in adversity* because he knew that action learners working in sets could build the networks to support each other through the risks and dangers that are part of the job of tackling significantly difficult problems.

Chapter summary

- Action learning works in sets and offers individuals space, time and a framework for critical reflection.

- Set members are encouraged to explore the tensions, emotions and power dynamics that exist in their working practices.

- This approach to development helps participants to be aware of their own theories-in-use, emancipated *from the often unseen constraints of assumption, habit, precedent, coercion and ideology* (Carr and Kemmis 2009: 46).

- Action learning encourages people to value their own experiences, trust their own insights and have the confidence to develop their own theories about their practice.

- The output of critically reflective action learning is in helping people to create theory from a critical appraisal of their practice, and through their new thinking improve their practice.

FURTHER READING

Brookfield, S.D. (1987) *Developing Critical Thinkers: Challenging Adults to Explore Alternative Ways of Thinking and Acting.* San Francisco, CA: Jossey-Bass.

Pedler, M. and Abbott, C. (2013) *Facilitating Action Learning: A Practitioner's Guide.* London: McGraw Hill.

Pedler, M.J., Abbott, C., Brook, C. and Burgoyne, J. (2013) *Improving Social Work Practice Through Critically Reflective Action Learning.* London: Skills for Care.

Part 2
Context

Chapter 4
Social and emotional intelligence

Introduction

Action learning sets can help support you as a student, social worker or a manager to develop your own emotional and social intelligence and start to develop your own emotional resilience – arguably a requirement in the current context of uncertainty and change. Emotions affect the very core of our being, from our evolutionary impulses to survive and procreate to the higher functioning of reason, logic and decision making. We started to look into how emotions might impact on decision making in Chapter 2 and this chapter will expand on the emotional impact of social work practice and how action learning, in the right environment, can facilitate practitioners becoming socially and emotionally literate professionals.

Whilst there is certainly a need for cognitive processing in what we do as social workers, far more important is our understanding of our emotions in the work we do. In this chapter, we will explore broad aspects of neurophysiology to understand how emotions have great importance in the world of social work practice.

'Emotional intelligence' and 'social intelligence' are terms more frequently found in management and leadership circles, driving a focus less on rational and cognitive intelligence and more on how emotions, relationships and the unconscious parts of the brain impact on our abilities to communicate and

Table 4.1 Approaches to emotions

Bureaucracy on emotions	Modern neuroscience on emotions
Make us inefficient	Make us effective
Indicate weakness	Indicate strength
Interfere with good judgement	Facilitate good judgement
Distract us	Motivate us
Obstruct, or slow down, reasoning	Enhance, or speed up, reasoning
Allow arbitrariness and tyranny	Build trust and connection
Weaken neutrality	Activate ethical values
Inhibit the flow of objective data	Provide vital feedback
Complicate planning	Spark creativity and innovation
Undermine administration	Enhance leadership

relate to others (Morrison, 2007). You may have remembered the education you received at school or college as having an emphasis on remembering, logical thinking and 'cool' rational questions as a measure of success in exams.

Table 4.1 shows some of the views on emotions, with the first column identifying how organisations which are overly bureaucratic in nature may view emotions compared to what modern neuroscience tells us (Kramer, 2007: 215).

It appears that there is a conflict between how bureaucratic organisations may view emotional responses by their workforce and the evidence from what modern neuroscience can tell us, e.g. the contrast between exploring emotions as signs of weakness or signs of strength. We argue in this chapter that it is the multitude of emotional states that give rise to a variety of cognitive processes and behaviours in action learning sets that pave the course of action. We identify that stress is a barrier to learning and that those who feel stressed will have a higher burnout rate and perform poorly with service users and for the organisation generally. It is therefore imperative that teams and organisations get this area right so the necessary support and resiliencies are interwoven into the cultural fabric, where showing emotion and exploring emotion are professional, essential to decision making and judgements and critical to social work practice.

Stress in social work

If you reflect back on your time as a social worker and indeed as a child, teenager and adult, there will have been times when you felt stressed, worried or anxious. The mere thought of reflecting back on a time when you have been stressed is probably enough to raise your heart rate a little and cause you to feel the effects of the human stress response. The nature of social work across both adults and children has the clear potential to create scenarios that induce high levels of stress, sickness and 'burnout' (Morrison, 2007).

Community Care's survey in 2009 of 450 social workers gives us a sense of what this reality looks like (Lombard, 2009). Their research found:

- Nearly three-quarters (72 per cent) face burnout due to making difficult decisions under stress.

- One in six always make tough decisions under pressure.

- One in ten *rarely* has access to adequate resources and support to inform practice.

- A third believes their supervision is inadequate.

A recent British Association of Social Workers (BASW) publication of *Professional Social Work* highlighted a University of Bedfordshire study. It noted that there were higher stress levels for those who wore their 'heart on their sleeve'. It further posited that employers need to do more to prevent burnout, including the need to understand the demands of the job, from working with people who have pain and suffering to the bureaucracy entrenched in all that goes with it. The career 'life expectancy', it was recorded, is a mere eight years (BASW, 2013).

In social work, there are difficult and complex decisions to be made, often in times of high pressure, whether this is from a particularly demanding or vulnerable service user or family member or from managers who are overly focused on performance, tick boxes and quantitative determinants of success. Indeed, it could be argued that helping people in stressful times is in itself stressful and endemic to social work practice (Howe, 2008). As we briefly explored in Chapter 2, part of the support that is assumed in professional social work practice is quality, regular supervision that facilitates the educational, social and emotional elements of practice so that decision making is shared and robust. However, firstly it is argued that this is not enough for some social workers who operate more effectively in group situations and for those who have a poor relationship with their supervisor. Critically, there should not be reliance or an assumption that supervisors and managers have the necessary emotional and social skills or time in a current culture of caseload management, budgetary controls and structural organisational changes. Therefore, current systems in place which are assumed to support social workers can only be relied upon where there is high-quality and regular supervision that does not simply focus on the caseload management and the performance agenda, but more on developing emotional wellbeing.

PRACTICE EXAMPLE

Recently, we facilitated a series of action learning sets for senior social workers and almost all of the issues and problems raised by the problem holders had their roots in emotional issues that caused some level of stress, resulting in decision making being a more difficult prospect. Initially, the set found it difficult to talk

PRACTICE EXAMPLE *continued*

about how they felt and overly focused on the 'thinking' of the issue. This meant that they had not integrated thought and feeling and most became stuck in moving the issue along. However, as the set developed and fresh questioning was perceived as helpful rather than a threat (something that more than likely elicited a stress response), the very nature of being listened to and having unequivocal space gave permission for all sorts of emotional states, previously not aroused, to be felt.

(Social work manager)

It appeared in those sets that the very nature of being stressed actually stopped them perceivably feeling anything. When trust was developed in the group and emotions were freely discussed, the set developed their understanding about how they became stressed and anxious and how this affected their ability to learn about the situation. Importantly, it also allowed them to feel human again, when the notion of being a 'professional social worker' was far more important to them initially. The belief that professionalism means that one should not show emotion at all costs is of concern to social work, particularly at a time of rapid change. It seems the idea of professionalism has been confused with managerialism. Revans's principle holds true that, where the rate of change exceeds the rate of learning, organisations are in trouble (Revans, 2011). Translated at the individual level, where the rate of change exceeds our abilities to understand and deal with complex issues and problems (which have their roots in emotions rather than simply cognitive rational processes), social workers are likely to feel stressed and overwhelmed and eventually succumb to sickness and 'burnout'. As we saw in Chapter 3, organisations 'cradled in anxiety' can impact heavily on the emotional wellbeing of individuals.

REFLECTION POINT

Reflect back to a time when you had to make an important decision in work or in your personal life.

- *How did you make this decision – on your own or with others?*

- *How were you feeling at the time? Was it a positive or negative experience?*

- *Do you think that your feelings impacted on your decision making and, if so, in what way?*

- *What did you learn about how you make decisions?*

- *Have you changed what you do as a result of this experience?*

Feeling challenged and pressured at work can be exciting and even exhilarating. These emotions can help develop our skills in managing high-risk situations and complex social work activity. However, when this challenge or pressure exceeds our ability to cope and we become overwhelmed, stress is likely to ensue, making the social work task a difficult, if not impossible, one. The action learning set can allow for a supportive environment and counter the threat and stress. The role in supporting others is identified in Chapter 8 and is critical to action learning.

Science of emotion

The human brain is probably the most complex and least understood organ on earth. However, modern-day neuroscience and some formative and arguably less ethical experiments have given way to a degree of understanding about how emotions/feelings and reasoning or cognitive processes interact. Whilst there is little intention and scope for this book to go into the intricacies of neuroscience, it is worth considering how the brain broadly operates in order to understand how cognitive processing and emotional states are so intertwined. In doing so, you will start to understand how we learn, make decisions and take actions by becoming aware of the emotional and cognitive areas of the brain.

Damasio (2006: 72) identifies in one study that in a woman who had a stroke, subsequent damage to the medial and dorsal areas of the frontal lobe region of the brain affected various neural functions and behaviour. The result of the stroke initially gave expressionless and unanimated behaviour with associated akinesia (reduced physical movement). As time progressed, with some active rehabilitation, the woman was able to convey her state of mind at that time and she recalled simply that she *had nothing to say*. Here the stroke affected her processing and emotional state so it was not that her communication had been solely a problem. Studies into parts of the brain that have been damaged offer some insight into the parts of the brain that affect cognitive processes and emotional states, both of which are highly intertwined with one another (Howe, 2008: 82). Arguably, it is important for us as social workers to understand some neuroscience because our questions, behaviours and projections will have an emotional impact on the arousal of others. For example, if our body language is confronting or our tone of voice is harsh and critical, it is more probable than not that the person will become defensive and even become in a state of 'fight or flight'. Also, it is important as social workers to become aware of our own emotional states so we can respond and process these behaviours in helpful ways so that there is less chance of confrontation and more chance of success in our interventions with adults, children and families.

The amygdala is considered to be part of the limbic system of the brain. It has the primary role in the processing of memory and emotional reactions. It receives stimuli from the outside world through the eyes and ears and information can bypass the cortex part of the brain (which deals with the higher cognitive functions). Howe (2008) argues that from an evolutionary point of view this is important as the thinking part of the brain is relatively slow. Thus, an immediate sense of danger can be registered as fear and an immediate reaction can take place. Much research into childhood trauma and distress has been affiliated with poor regulation of emotions and such experiences cause physical changes to the human brain. The 'emotional memory' part of the brain has been singled out here for a reason because social workers need to be aware that their own memories of distress, trauma or poor childhood experiences may at times, and in particular when stressed, cause an immediate behavioural response which is not thought through or necessarily understood, i.e. it remains outside our awareness. If we translate these ideas to the service users and families who, as has already been asserted, often come into social workers' lives because of their emotional trauma and poor experiences in life, their emotional 'radar' will be highly receptive to your emotional and behavioural stimulus and responses.

CASE STUDY 4.1

Action learning sets offer a chance to speak about challenges and problems and how these make us feel. Last year, we were facilitating an action learning set for newly qualified social workers and one member of the group had difficulties with a particular supervisor with whom she had a poor working relationship. This meant that the social worker felt unable to ask the supervisor questions and it felt 'unsafe' when speaking with the supervisor. The supervisor was described as 'scary' and 'aggressive' in approach. The practitioner had identified that when she spoke with the supervisor, her heart rate notably increased, her palms became sweaty and her cheeks were flushed. It seems that a stress response was taking place and, because of this feeling, the practitioner became stuck, often actively avoiding the supervisor or becoming passive in her interactions. The relationship was described as 'dysfunctional' and 'toxic' and the social worker dreaded the idea of coming into work. It was becoming so problematic that the social worker had correlated her time working with the supervisor with an increased rate of sickness.

The action learning set supported the social worker in understanding the issue better, and, importantly, in a safe environment where emotions could be spoken about. It took a while for the set to feel comfortable enough to talk about how they felt, but once a degree of trust was established, the powerful ways in which emotional states and thinking processes were linked appeared to result in better action planning and, crucially, increased motivation to problem solve. It also meant that the social worker could put the situation in context and understand her emotional responses better and actually empowered her to become increasingly assertive and confident. One of the actions from the set was for the social worker to generate an agenda for the next supervision session and one of the agenda items was for 'feedback'.

Because the social worker had modelled some of the feedback in the set (almost like a dress rehearsal!), she felt more confident about the purpose of the feedback and rather than act on impulse and stress, gave feedback to the supervisor in a non-confrontational, non-aggressive and assertive way. In doing so, she was less likely to arouse a stress response from the supervisor and enter into any psychological game playing (Berne, 1964). At the next action learning set, the actions were reviewed and reflected upon. The social worker had said that she felt 'liberated' and 'relieved' and her relationship with her supervisor was actually stronger than with some of her other work colleagues! The relationship was described as 'real' and 'genuine'.

(Action learning facilitator)

Becoming emotionally aware and having the confidence and behaviours to manage this situation proved helpful not just with her supervisor but when working with service users and other professionals. It is also helpful to look beyond the rational and task-oriented nature of traditional action learning approaches. Issues of power and politics in action learning are as important as looking at the problem or challenge; it allows the problem holder to view the issue in context, which invariably has explicit power attached to it or around it. We looked into power and politics more explicitly in Chapter 3.

Becoming 'emotionally intelligent'

What appears to be important is to be in at the birth of a new insight, not necessarily one's own, when there bursts forth that gasp of surprise which reveals that, at last, somebody has suddenly seen a new relationship that brings new perspectives to his world.

Revans (1982: 603)

As we have seen already, in England, social workers are now required to evidence their 'capabilities' through the Professional Capabilities Framework (PCF) and an integral part of how this is assessed is through holistic assessment. However, despite some mention in the PCF, this needs further exploration to ensure that social workers are not becoming *practitioner technicians* (Morrison, 2007). Banks (1995) many years ago realised the cultural shift in social work towards managerialism. Social workers are far more than form fillers, risk and care managers; they are agents of change in the lives of the most vulnerable in society. In order to fulfil this requirement, being a 'change agent' means that social workers need to have skills that go far beyond the bureaucratic technical-rational activities promoted by successive central policy units.

The human interaction between social worker and service user continues to be a core social work skill. Gaining rapport, understanding and empathy supports social change which requires emotionally and socially competent practitioners at the heart of this process. Whether completing assessments, advocacy, care planning or problem solving, the inability of social workers to understand the

61

emotional states of others, and their own, can lead to decisions which are overly based on procedural or linear decision making and devoid of the emotional and social dynamic in the relationship. As Howe argues:

> *Social work and social care are essentially relationship-based practices even if many of the explicit techniques and statutory demands impose more formal rules of engagement. Relationships can only be conducted with skill and compassion if the worker is emotionally intelligent.*

(Howe, 2008: 181)

Action learning sets are helpful in developing social workers to become agents of change with one another; supporting *comrades in adversity* to overcome feeling 'stuck' in their learning. Much of the set is concerned with problem solving and it is reported that the 'felt shift' in perspective, which is required for real change, requires set members to question the feelings and emotions of the problem holder. In modelling these questions in a relatively safe environment, social work practitioners and managers can learn to be competent at the type of questions asked as well as using their emotional and social intelligence to monitor their emotions and those of others in the process. Central to Goleman's (1998) definition of emotional intelligence is the notion of being able to control impulses and to delay gratification.

A drive towards solution-focused interventions is not entirely congruent with emotionally or socially intelligent practice. Action learning set members can find it easy to go straight to the answer of the problem and treat it as a puzzle rather than a wicked problem, without careful exploration, reflection and questioning. By answering the question on behalf of set members, this becomes not only disempowering for the problem holder; it also reduces any hope of learning about the problem or themselves. Emotionally, it may help to solve their anxiety as the 'rescuer' but ultimately, it is argued here that the problem holder may feel frustrated and disempowered in the process. Reducing the impulse for answers and gratification supports listening skills, patience and faith in the problem holder to get to a point where new perspectives can be viewed through a different lens.

As we saw in Chapter 2, reflection can occur at different levels and can support a shift in belief systems and support the idea of *transformational learning* (Mezirow, 1991). Action learning sets can provide a place of trust and safety that allows the sort of reflection that is difficult to achieve in the current and largely unsatisfactory models of supervision available to social workers. Being able to reflect on core beliefs and motivations is at the heart of our thinking and action. Without understanding the feelings beneath what it is that makes us react or delay, act or not act and enthused or bored supports the uncovering of hidden feelings of being scared, excited, frightened and anxious – to name just a few of the emotions that can be articulated here.

Thus, it is not enough simply to reflect on the patterns and phenomena in our social work interventions. Instead there is a requirement for deep understanding and critical reflection of the emotions, power and assumptions we have, all of which need exploration and uncovering from our unconsciousness, from where a lot of decisions are directed. Revans (2011: 74) argues that *there are, of course, many who go on doing the same ineffectual things all their life, and at the end of it they attract the comment: There's no fool like an old fool.* For Revans, taking aboard new belief systems or, as Bateson (1972) defined as our *epistemology*, might be painful and mean that we stop ourselves from learning and shifting behaviours, thinking and feeling because they contradict established views and accepted traditions.

ACTIVITY 4.1

On a large piece of plain paper, write down the term 'Emotional and social intelligence' and write what this term means to you (and others) individually or in a group, in the form of a tree with branches coming from the central trunk.

What does it feel like to be emotionally and socially competent – what does it look like? How would you know if you were? What skills are required?

Finally, critically reflect on what stops social workers becoming emotionally and socially competent, particularly in relation to power, politics, economics and society.

This can be done in a larger group (of up to 100 people!) using a very large piece of paper and individual groups can be used to draw on ideas that can be connected to form a web of patterns and understanding between themes.

Becoming 'socially intelligent'

Working co-operatively with others in social work has become enshrined in law, policy and principles of best practice. We will look more closely at working in the multi-agency context in Chapter 6 but for now, we focus on what it means to be socially intelligent. This concept is arguably inextricably linked to emotional intelligence because, without the self-control, impulse regulation and motivation, it would be very difficult to become socially literate in understanding others' emotions and problems. In action learning sets, being able to ask good questions is very helpful at triggering the thoughts and feelings of the problem holder. By being able to assess verbal and non-verbal cues and develop rapport in a group, the problem holder is far more likely to work through the issue and in doing so become motivated to take action – an essential ingredient for successful action learning sets. In the social work context, Howe asserts that group work is invaluable to promote social and emotional intelligence:

The risk for those whose emotional intelligence is underdeveloped is an increase in social isolation. Those who are lonely experience more stress and poor health. Some of the benefits of group support and therapeutic group work lie in the raised positive emotions that can be experienced when we feel connected and understood by others.

(Howe, 2008: 115)

Being able to build rapport with service users can be a tricky task, not least because the individual may be socially isolated or may have experienced emotional/ physical trauma that stops him or her from wanting to engage with social workers. The importance of understanding our power, whether actual or perceived, cannot be understated here and what you do as a social worker in your interactions with service users can be the difference between real genuine change and complete disengagement. Developing your skills to empathise with their experience and showing emotional 'warmth' in your tone of language and body language will go some way towards reducing the likelihood of stress responses and improve how you connect emotionally and socially.

PRACTICE EXAMPLE

A social worker recently commented after an action learning set meeting that she honestly did not feel connected with some of her service users. It caused her a lot of heartache because she began to wonder whether she was up to the job and felt emotionally dissatisfied. She considered whether she could bring this problem to the next action learning set. Despite her relative lack of motivation, she did so, and started to realise that she was not connecting to certain service users because she perceived them as threatening but had not consciously made the connection between their behaviour, her feelings and then her avoidance and dissatisfaction. The social worker learnt not only about service users in more depth and appreciated why they might feel threatened and became aggressive at times but also new strategies to improve rapport with service users and to understand her own emotional regulation. Furthermore, the avoidant strategies had worked against the social worker because the service user no longer trusted that she was reliable (as the previous two social workers had also not been).

(Social work manager)

Offering feedback to colleagues, service users and their carers is an activity in social work that often receives less attention than it deserves. Feedback to others is a necessary and important social work task and helps us to develop social literacy. If undertaken using the appropriate linguistics and intentions, feedback can improve practice, motivate individuals and support the emotional and social development of others. Race, as cited by Williams and Rutter (2010: 76), argues for a model that includes motivational elements (wanting and needing) as part of the feedback process, rather than the overly technical staged approach of Kolb's (1984) model. Action learning sets provide a platform and a safety net for supportive and challenging feedback to take place between set members and for this to become part of a culture of 'what goes on around here' rather than the annual appraisal culture with limited and technical feedback. When offering support and empathy to set members, and of course service users, you *boldly swing into the life of another* (Buber, 1965, cited in Brockbank and McGill, 2004).

REFLECTION POINT

- *How well are you connected with others, including family, friends, professionals and service users on your caseload?*

- *What are your strengths when it comes to making connections and building rapport with others?*

- *Which areas do you think you could improve upon and what benefits will this bring to your relationships?*

Action learning sets are a way of connecting with others to achieve more than in other group meetings. Because the focus is on the problem holder, the set can work together in asking fresh questions that stimulate the emotional and social centres of the brain so that sense can be made of a situation which may initially seem quite logical and cold and yet, actually, the breadth and depth of the problem lie in powerful emotions and relationships. Therefore action learning does not operate in a tight vacuum of empty emotions; instead it thrives on them and they can help to motivate, excite and create action outside the learning set. Kurt Lewin (1951: 229) identified that *it is sometimes necessary to bring about deliberately an emotional stir up*. Equally, the turbulence of emotions can be quite overwhelming and the skill of the facilitator (who will also need a good helping of emotional intelligence) will be tested for sets who are emotionally impulsive and who lack drive and focus. As a social worker, you will encounter service users and families who may come with their own collective and individual emotions. How you begin to understand them in their situation will come down to how well you understand yourself emotionally and how, in turn, you connect with them to create a safe basis for change and real-time problem solving.

Chapter summary

- Social workers need to develop emotional resilience and 'intelligence' which, in the right conditions, can be nurtured through action learning sets; highly emotionally intelligent sets maintain focus and keep going when they are challenged and are able to delay gratification in pursuit of social problem solving.

- Emotions are highly intelligent and, whilst they might be ignored by some managers and organisations which resort to method and process to solve problems, the real issues and problems for service users have their roots in emotional dysregulation, anxiety and emotional trauma.

- Overly processed and formulaic systems in social work that advocate for procedure, bureaucratism and managerialism over intuition can cause stress on top of the day-to-day practice of working with distressed and vulnerable children and adults.

- Learning in sets can cause some members feelings of anxiety; developing our emotional self and reducing this anxiety will likely minimise stress responses which inhibit learning and understanding.

- Developing our ability to respond to others' needs as much as our own is an important skill for social workers to develop rapport, increase trust and facilitate the change; action learning sets facilitate social workers to become socially literate where modelling, creative practice and real-time problem solving can be explored more safely.

- Current systems of casework supervision do not go far enough in ensuring that social workers are supported in a role which demands complex decision making in a context of continual change and emotional stressors.

- Becoming emotionally resilient is not straightforward and, it is argued, is best supported in action learning sets, where high degrees of trust and challenge can ensure that set members feel safer and more readily able to assert their emotions and problem-solving abilities.

- On top of all other skills and requisites for professional social work practice it is therefore crucial and absolutely desirable for social workers to have an understanding of their emotions and those of others so that they have higher degrees of success in their interventions.

FURTHER READING

Damasio, A. (2006) *Descartes' Error*. London: Picador Vintage.

Goleman, D. (1998) *Working with Emotional Intelligence*. London: Bloomsbury.

Howe, D. (2008) *The Emotionally Intelligent Social Worker*. Hampshire: Palgrave Macmillan.

Chapter 5

Anti-discriminatory practice and anti-oppressive practice

Introduction

This chapter will focus on anti-discriminatory and anti-oppressive practice in social work, with a special focus on working in action learning sets. We will argue that the power of questioning (Q) will allow you to start questioning your assumptions about your own personal and professional values in a safe environment using action learning as the driving methodology. As we have already seen in Chapter 3, understanding power relations and the bigger social picture rather than just the individual view can help us as social workers see the world with a more critical lens. We argue in this chapter that challenging assumptions and questioning where power lies and where discrimination and oppression exist are the building blocks to genuine emancipation.

> one of the main priorities of the social work profession is 'the liberation of people to enhance well-being'.
>
> (International Federation of Social Workers, 2002)

In Chapter 1 we noted the similarities between the Quaker beliefs of Revans and action learning, acknowledging that *action learning . . . starts in 'not knowing'*, or as Revans said: *unless we understand and acknowledge our own ignorance in the face of difficult problems, then we are not able to seek questions and learning* (Pedler and Abbott 2013: 14).

As social workers, we are often faced with very difficult questions to ask, not just of ourselves but also of management structures that stifle emancipatory action and instead develop cultures of oppression and discrimination. We are also challenged with questioning the belief systems and values of service users and families, whether this is with an older person with prejudiced views of Black or Asian people or of younger generations of children and teenagers who view women or homosexual people in derogatory ways. Societal values are much stronger than we might think, relative to our own individual values, and this will be looked at more closely throughout this chapter to help you start to think about your individual beliefs and values in the context of society.

Social workers are not practising in isolation; rather they are practising in systems which often have different values and sets of belief systems, underpinned by a variety of assumptions, and this creates power, tension and discrimination to others. Social work has a role to play in society, with a bold aim to break down this oppression and liberate service user power so they can become autonomous and self-actualising members of society. Clearly this is a vision which cannot always be realised, especially when the organisation that you work in may not have the same vision. As we continue through this chapter, we will explore how action learning in your organisation may help to support a change in culture, right to the top of the management structure. As Revans stated, *doubt ascending speeds wisdom above* (cited in Pedler, 2012: 13). The final part of this chapter will ask you those difficult and challenging questions about what your organisation encourages, discourages and actively avoids and what culture this establishes, one of learning or one of maintaining the status quo.

Anti-oppressive practice

Power is everywhere; not because it embraces everything, but because it comes from everywhere.

(Foucault, 1998: 93 cited in Paechter, 1998: 55)

Anti-oppressive practice can be thought of as *a process of change which leads [service users] from feeling powerless to powerful* (Dalrymple and Burke, 1995). Dominelli (1993) argues that anti-oppressive practice is person-centred and concerned with challenging structural inequality and hierarchical systems of power. Developed almost exclusively in social work, it is a *dominant theory to critical social work practice* (Healy, 2005: 178). Thus, we are concerned as social workers not only about individual power relations but also about the structural and political nature of practice in the wider context of organisations, culture and society.

Social workers are faced with difficult situations, often, as we have seen in Chapter 4, heaped in emotional distress, caused by a number of issues, including disability, discrimination, poverty, illness, and so on. Whether you are practising as a hospital social worker looking to facilitate a safe discharge for an older person or assessing and supporting a child through child protection proceedings, the aim is arguably the same: to increase the power that they have as individuals so they can feel 'empowered'. The word 'empowerment' is quite a loaded (and often overused and misunderstood) term used by social policy units and frameworks aimed at reducing oppression and discrimination but with little pragmatic methodology at the practitioner level. It is for this reason that we discuss anti-oppressive practice in this book, because of the realities of social work that do not currently lend themselves towards genuine emancipation.

We argue that this is in part due to the grip of increasing bureaucracy and managerialism which limits our own power to effect real change. Action learning sets can give us this opportunity to become 'change agents' and offer fresh questioning and action that then give practitioners the opportunity not only for reflective practice but also reflexive practice in real time. It is this reflexive action or maybe, put more simply, understanding the uniqueness of each individual, that sets it apart from reflection on individual practice and, instead, gives insight into how we as individuals are the many parts that make up cultures, organisations and society. Importantly for anti-oppressive practice, these states are never static, whether this is due to social, economic or political changes in government or more widely in society; reflexive social work practice is fluid and dynamic (Burke and Dalrymple, 2000). Revans (2011) on action learning supports the constancy of external change and, where organisations cannot keep up with this rate of external change, dire consequences are to follow: rate of learning $\geq$ rate of change $=$ survival ($L \geq C$).

We argue here that it is not enough in anti-oppressive practice to reflect, analyse and pontificate about the injustices we face. It requires (sober and deliberate) action to challenge the personal, cultural and structural injustices which can later be reflected upon critically in action learning sets.

Figure 5.1 demonstrates how oppression can be analysed at different levels.

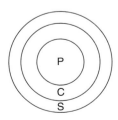

Figure 5.1 Analysis of oppression (adapted from Thompson's (2009) PCS model)

In this model Thompson highlights three levels: P, personal, C, cultural and S, structural:

1. *P* represents the personal level where the individual holds the belief system, prejudice or value, e.g. a male holding sexist views about females. This can also be thought of as the 'psychological' level.

2. *C* represents the shared beliefs in cultures which are an *assumed consensus of what is normal*, e.g. all females are unable to carry out manual labour.

3. *S* represents the structural views and Thompson here makes explicit that at this level, *oppression and discrimination are institutionalised and thus 'sewn in' to the fabric of society* (Thompson, 2009: 19).

At the centre of this model is the person, arguably something that as social workers we overly focus on to effect change. For example, in a hospital environment it is all too tempting to look at the person's diagnosis, individual strengths and weaknesses and even become consumed by a medical model which seeks to treat and cure. As Strier (2007: 858) asserts, *Social work is a profession highly conditioned by institutional inequalities*. These individual areas of focus can be helpful to look at but critically, it is the context and social situation which are rarely thought about, often because legislation, cultures of rapid hospital discharge and reducing numbers of hospital beds do not allow time for such 'luxury'. However, for the service user (or patient) in a hospital environment, the culture, structure and the overuse of 'expert power' by health and social work practitioners can be a frightening and daunting journey. Social workers in such an environment must therefore become acutely aware of their role in these situations. Challenging 'expert' health professionals, advocacy supporting a person-centred approach and where the voice of the person can genuinely be heard and highlighting to policy makers the requirements for change are a few of the many roles of anti-oppressive practice. All of these roles are aimed at increasing the power for service users and reducing oppression. Action learning sets can support such change, where individual action alone might not be enough. Through collective action which might emerge from challenges brought to light by an individual set member, the group may decide to support radical change. This of course requires time, commitment and motivation.

REFLECTION POINT

It is helpful to undertake this piece of reflection using a learning journal or some paper to write down your reflections.

- *Can you think back to a challenge you have had as a social worker when you acted, maybe at a time of adversity, against the prevailing decision making of another professional, service user or family member?*

- *What did it feel like to be in this position?*

- *Who had the power and how was it used by others and by you?*

- *Which people in your scenario were, in your view, less powerful or more oppressed by the presenting situation?*

- *What did you do and what did others do in relation to your action?*

- *How did the challenge conclude (if indeed it did) in terms of the shift in power (if at all)?*

Anti-discriminatory practice

We have seen how anti-oppressive practice can be practised in action learning to solve real-time problems which have issues embedded in structural, cultural or personal oppression. The lack of power you may feel as a social worker can be transformed through a supportive set so that *participants become encouraged to explore what they cannot see around them as well as what they imagine they can* (Revans, 2011: 10).

Anti-discriminatory practice involves strategies and action to minimise and combat discrimination. Discrimination can lead to oppression, disadvantage and disempowerment and so there are close links with anti-oppressive practice. Power clearly has a role in discrimination and it is argued that those with greater power, whether this is political, professional, personal or otherwise, are likely to cause the greatest impact on those who have less power. There can of course be situations where positive discrimination is helpful in some situations, e.g. an action learning set that has six males and no females might be seen as gender-imbalanced and lacking a diverse range of experiences. Another example could be that there are eight social workers who are of the same age and from similar backgrounds and have the same challenges and issues. Arguably, each will come with a uniqueness of experience and cultures but the diversity of issues may well be different and so consideration into membership of any group including learning sets is required. Pedler and Abbott consider the diversity of an action learning set and ask the question: *who should be the set members*?

> *A key design parameter is: is there enough diversity of participants to give rise to fresh questions? This is a matter of judgement. There are many sources of diversity amongst people to be considered in any action learning design.*

> (Pedler and Abbott, 2013: 49)

When taking part in an action learning set, it is helpful to ask the question of commonality, difference and diversity as they will potentially give rise to some interesting reflections on your own learning about who you are and how you fit into the group and more widely into the social fabric of society. These are critical questions and will help to see which lens and perspective you view the world through and, crucially, what values are important to you when analysing situations, taking action and making decisions.

In terms of legislation, historically there were a number of statutory frameworks regarding discrimination. However, the Equality Act (2010) has combined a number of separate pieces of legislation into one, which covers nine characteristics which cannot be used to treat others unfairly:

1. race;

2. age;

3. disability;

4. gender reassignment;

5. marriage and civil partnership;

6. pregnancy and maternity;

7. religion or belief;

8. sex;

9. sexual orientation.

This differs then to oppression which, although inextricably linked to discrimination, does not have a legal framework underpinning it. What is important to realise here is that, whilst legislation governs these nine characteristics and we would argue that this is helpful, there is a lot still to be done as social workers. There are a number of complex issues and challenges that face service users and for social workers involved in their lives. It is not as simple as it first seems for statute to be passed and for perfect harmony to be created where discrimination is eradicated from society. Service user liberation and emancipation continue to require challenge from those with a critical lens on the matter and to ask the questions which confront the prevailing ideology and cultural and societal norms.

ACTIVITY **5.1**

Using the complexity mapping process, use the theories of anti-discriminatory practice and anti-oppressive practice which can be written in the centre of a large piece of paper (if possible, around 5m by 2m) to highlight the emerging themes of the group. The group can be very large, with unlimited numbers, to generate a wide range of diverse views which are affecting anti-oppressive or anti-discriminatory social work practice.

Different types of power

Power comes in different forms and, as we have already seen, oppression and discrimination occur at different levels, from the personal to the structural. A further question is: what types of power are there? We argue here that it is useful for social work practitioners to label (although labels often have negative connotations and hidden assumptions) certain powers so they can be discussed and opened up in action learning sets for debate and challenge. French and Raven (1959) argue that there are five bases of power:

1. legitimate;

2. reward;

3. expert;

4. referent;

5. coercive.

As a social worker, you will have a certain type of power that you exert (e.g. legitimate, professional etc.) and other powers that are exerted upon you from external influences, e.g. cultural norms ('how things are done around here'). In action learning sets, power exists relationally between group members and from the outside world, i.e. the organisation, politics, economics. There is a tension of power created between the individuals and the wider systems in which the set operates. The problem or challenge must therefore be seen in a context of power that impacts on the feelings, thoughts and actions taken by set members. It is argued here that the sets provide a relative safety net for exploration and challenge of power, whether this is seen as 'legitimate', which has assumptions hidden beneath the legitimacy, or coercive and potentially more abusive powers that are possibly more overt and free for every set member to see. Because cultural norms are so strong and influential, it might be very difficult to swim against the normative tide of influence. However, ignoring these subtle and not so subtle cultural norms is dangerous and requires an enquiring set of questions to expose the power hidden at different levels of challenge and opportunity.

As we saw in Chapter 4, set members who are engaged with their emotions and who socially understand their 'position' in a group are more likely to develop higher levels of trust and collaboration. Moreover, there is a greater chance for set members to become aware of the political power, which may lead to new insights and, crucially, new learning (McGill and Beaty, 2001). Despite this optimism in understanding, recognising and challenging the power that exists all around us, there are still criticisms of social work, often from the far left, who view social workers as 'agents of the state'. The challenge for children social work is explored by Okitikpi:

> *The tension for practitioners in this climate is how to intervene earlier in order to prevent abuse and at the same time build rapport and develop the necessary relationship with the children and their families. In essence practitioners are expected to exercise their powers while at the same time not be discriminatory, judgmental or infringe on aspects of the human rights acts that relate to the children and their families.*

> (Okitikpi, 2011: 9)

Of course the same dilemmas are experienced across all sectors of social work from youth work to mental health and social work with older people. Action learning is therefore suggested as a powerful tool and a way of working with your colleagues, with service users and families to reframe social work power, explore discrimination at multiple levels of society and promote genuine empowerment in the process. How power and discrimination can be implemented in action learning is explored now by looking at the power of *Q* in Revans's learning equation $L = P + Q$. Importantly, it is asserted here that it is *Q* that will provide new insights and perspectives rather than *P*, which is knowledge *already out there* (Pedler, 2008; Revans, 2011).

The power of questioning (*Q*)

For Revans, the key area of learning is in the fresh questioning that takes place about what we do not know and about what we do not already have solutions for (Pedler and Abbott, 2013). For Revans, the programmed knowledge already out there in the world and in text books was only as good as the day it was written because of the changing environment in which knowledge is created. We have already explored social work's adapting landscape and its struggle to keep up with the rate of legislative, socio-political and economic change. In view of these multi-faceted dimensions of change and the power that this brings to teams, organisations and cultures, the critical role of questioning insight (*Q*) becomes evident.

In action learning, those sets that have high degrees of challenge in questioning the problem holder are arguably more likely to stir the emotional and cognitive parts of the brain into action. However, as we have seen in Chapter 4 on emotional and social intelligence, stress responses (with the accompanying release of cortisol) are likely to reduce creativity and cognitive processing; instead, automatic and pre-programmed responses will become the problem holder's subjective experience. Therefore a balance of critical and fresh questioning coupled with a large helping of support as *comrades in adversity* is likely to create an environment of learning.

Understanding the power of questioning will help you as set members, as a facilitator and as a social worker to develop skills in becoming critically reflective. The questioning of assumptions, power relations between people, organisations and community is argued here as a requirement to develop anti-oppressive and anti-discriminatory practice. It is simply not enough to have the knowledge of the law or some social work theory if you are not going to question how laws, policies, theories and models have developed. As we have also posited, an environment where the questioning of 'how things are done around here' is a necessity, not just in action learning sets but in the wider organisational setting. Supervision, as has been suggested earlier, for the most part has not created a sufficient environment to reflect critically on processes which generate and sustain oppressive and discriminative practice. Heavy emphasis on case work management and a culture of moving cases on using solution-focused remedies is a dangerous proposition for practitioners walking the tightrope between risk and self-determination. In the next case study, we can see how a social worker in adult services made a number of assumptions about a service user and how the set challenged these assumptions, exposing the powers of the individual and the organisation she worked for.

CASE STUDY **5.1**

In one action learning set that was facilitated in 2011, a social worker had identified that she was struggling to work with a service user who she had assessed and undertaken a support plan with. The service user was 82 years old, male, white and had few support networks and little income. The challenge for the social worker was that she felt that the service user was 'difficult', 'obstructive' and too 'demanding of her time' and that there were no services that could meet his needs. After some questioning by the set members, it became apparent that the issue was not with the service user, but with the assumptions and power she had taken with her to the assessment and the power she then took away from him. The set engaged the social worker to think about her values and what elements of the service user's behaviour were 'difficult' and 'challenging'. As time went on, with a further round of questions, the social worker identified that it was her own struggle to complete the social work assessment satisfactorily because the form did not allow for key elements of the service user's life to be included, causing much frustration for the service user and behaviour that challenged the social worker (to the point where she was visibly anxious and distressed).

The social worker redefined her problem, which transpired to be about the organisation and the assumptions she had made about the social work panel's decision making. On reflection, the social worker relived a stressful experience of trying to get through what she felt was a reasonable request for additional care. The panel (which included two senior managers) refused the application for additional care and had responded to the social worker in an abrupt manner and criticised the application on several grounds. As the action learning set progressed, using a five-step model, the set members asked questions about the power and culture of the organisation:

- *How did you feel when your application was turned down by the panel?*

- *Are there accepted scenarios where the panel does readily fund additional care, without question?*

- *On reflection, what have you assumed about this service user in relation to the other service user?*

- *Does the management team encourage creative personalisation?*

- *How can you challenge the social care panel next time?*

- *What power do you think you have with this service user?*

- *What power did the social care panel have when you last applied for funding?*

The social worker stated that she had several 'light bulb moments' about her practice and that of her organisation. She determined that the issue actually was

CASE STUDY **5.1** *continued*

with the relationship quality between her and one of the managers on the social work panel. She decided to take action on this challenge by bringing it up in her next supervision, creating an agenda prior to the supervision and actively discussing how she felt about the power imbalances in this case and the culture of decision making in the panel and more widely in the organisation.

(Action learning facilitator)

From this case study, it appears evident that the social worker made real action in supervision to readdress the power issues she faced not only with the organisation but with service users and colleagues, gaining assertiveness in her practice. In this sense, the set genuinely provided a launch pad for emancipatory action which rocketed her towards challenge and liberation. Without the support and challenge from set members to engage critically with her issue, it would have been difficult, if not impossible, to realise fully the underlying powers and oppression at different levels, from the personal to the assumed consensus of the social care panel (Thompson, 1997). It would be an assumption to believe now that this social worker continued her efforts to liberate herself from the powers of the funding panels and the organisation. However, continued support, action and critical reflection on action in learning sets give new optimism towards liberating anti-oppressive and anti-discriminatory practice.

REFLECTION POINT

- *What in particular did you relate to in this scenario?*
- *Reflecting on your own experience of groups (e.g. current groups that are already set up in your organisation, like team meetings), do they engage at the critically reflective and reflexive levels?*
- *What might be the advantages and disadvantages of challenging oppression and discrimination in your organisation?*

Reflexivity

Social work is a profession highly conditioned by institutional inequalities.

(Strier, 2007)

Reflexivity in social work has become increasingly significant, to look beyond *benign introspection* (Woolgar, 1988: 22). This benign introspection to describe what happens and view our thinking in relation to a particular scenario is argued as reflective practice. 'What happened? Who was there? What do you think went well?' are questions that require reflectivity and have a space in supervision and in learning about a problem or a situation. It is argued that reflexive practice goes further; it requires us to think about how our experience has shaped learning and thinking. Reflexivity therefore can consider ideas of power and difference and helps us to become 'ignorant' in the face of expertise. Reflexivity has been defined by Hassard (1993) and Taylor and White (2002), as cited by D'Cruz *et al.*, as:

> *An important practice skill and central to working ethically in uncertain contexts and unpredictable situations – as opposed to instrumental accountability (following rules and procedures):*
>
> - *Critical self-awareness by the practitioner, in how he or she understands and engages with social problems.*
>
> - *Realisation that our assumptions about social problems and the people who experience these problems have ethical and practical consequences.*
>
> - *Questioning of personal practice, knowledge and assumptions.*
>
> (D'Cruz et al., 2007: 77)

Furthermore, in the review of reflexivity by D'Cruz *et al.*, attention was also paid to looking beyond the rational, technical and cognitive aspects of the job and more towards the emotions that affect and transform practice. They comment:

> *The meanings of reflexivity generated by participants in our research also identified emotions as being an important part of the process of knowledge creation. Participants spoke of their emotional responses when they attempted to apply a critical approach to the generation of knowledge to guide their practice. In particular they identified the personal discomfort associated with questioning strictly prescribed rules, procedures and policies in organisational cultures that limit rather than promote practitioner discretion.*
>
> (D'Cruz et al., 2007: 83)

We argue that reflexive practice is ethical practice since it challenges the assumptions that procedure, policy and theory generate cultures of oppressive and discrimination. Action learning is a tool that can be used not just in discrete formal learning sets but in everyday practice to formulate new theories of reality and generate new knowledge from a position of ignorance. Understanding emotion and power and allowing space for introspection and analysis are parts of critical action learning that help support individual and organisational learning in powerful ways. Current systems and organisations that do not permit social workers to challenge and do not allow time for active challenge are at real risk because the rate of change externally will arguably impede the rate at which learning can take place. As we saw earlier from Revans's learning formula of $L \geq C$, for survival it is critically imperative of learning to keep up with this change (Revans, 2011).

Chapter summary

- Social workers require the skills, emotional intelligence and confidence to challenge oppression and discrimination. It has been argued that action learning provides a methodology to look critically at our practice and the culture of the organisation to ask difficult questions.

- Oppression and discrimination can occur at different levels, as we have seen with Thompson's (2009) PCS model.

- Engaging with problems using critical reflection involves much more than just analysis and description of what was perceived to go right or wrong. Instead, it requires a reflective approach that asks fresh questions in relation to politics, power and cultural norms as well as societal expectations on social workers.

- Emotional engagement with problems in action learning sets is as important as looking at the thinking and willing elements of an issue. Lots of the problems and issues where oppression and discrimination occur happen at this level and so to disengage with emotions is simply avoidant and must be challenged in sets.

- High levels of trust and challenge are a good recipe for learning in sets, which also provide a safety net for difficult and challenging questions to be asked.

- Without support, set members may feel uncertain about how well they can trust other set members and too little challenge may result in yet another meeting where everyone attempts to maintain the status quo and continues in a single loop of learning (Argyris and Schön, 1978).

- A diverse range of set members may help support understandings of difference in a safe context. Issues of race, gender, disablism and culturalism can be explored in action learning sets where questions are posed critically and not simply the problem, in a vacuum, devoid of power and oppression.

- Challenging power is not easy and there is still a lot to be done. However, with the support of colleagues and friends in times of adversity, lots can be done to shift the prevailing powers of oppression and discrimination as individuals, in organisations and in wider society.

FURTHER READING

Dominelli, L. (2002) *Anti-Oppressive Social Work Theory and Practice.* Basingstoke: Palgrave Macmillan.

Thompson, N. (2009) *Promoting Equality, Valuing Diversity.* Lyme Regis: Russell House Publishing.

Chapter 6

Involving other professions: multi-agency practice

Introduction

Multi-agency practice has been widely researched and written about in social work (Henwood *et al.*, 1997; Hudson, 2002; Brown *et al.*, 2003; Glasby, 2003; Glendinning, 2003; Gannon-Leary *et al.*, 2006; Morris, 2008). Furthermore, it is enshrined in statutory legislation as a duty for several areas of social work practice, spanning back to the 1968 Seebohm Report to the Children Act 2004 and Mental Health Act 2007, all stressing the requirement to promote co-operation with other agencies. Morrison (2007: 5) asserts that: *the importance of relationship skills extends beyond practitioner–user interactions, to working with other colleagues, disciplines and systems. Relationship competence is equally important for supervisors, administrators, leaders and managers.*

The continued interest in multi-agency practice for academics, practitioners and managers in social work suggests that collaboration may not be working as well as it could be. In this chapter, we will argue that multi-agency practice is a 'good thing' and we will explore how action learning can promote genuine collaboration across disciplines as a practical and powerful methodology. There will also be a section on how critical reflection and analysis can support better insights into notions of collaboration, partnership and professional identity. Taking a critical view is argued as helpful to ask difficult and challenging questions about power between professionals (both as individuals and as organisations and agencies). With the support of the learning set, health, social care and other professionals interested in getting down to some real-time action and learning can develop new insights and define new problems to work on.

Some of the many sets we have facilitated have raised a number of 'wicked problems' which are often associated with working with others, relationships or misunderstanding of roles. In turn, this has created hostile working environments and a rebuilding of the 'Berlin wall' that successive policies and best-practice initiatives have attempted to erode. Pullen-Sansfaçon and Ward (2012: 1) identify that true teamwork is stifled and *compounded in relation to inter-professional 'teams', by the top-down, prescriptive, policy drivers which have led to their setting-up and because of 'new managerialism' embedded in their operation.* It is posited that action learning is a practice that is sceptical of 'experts' and can begin to acknowledge and eliminate barriers between professionals by challenging the dominant normative cultures, where expertise and knowledge (P) are regarded as paramount over wisdom and the questioning of insight (Q). For example, hospitals, mental health units and courts are areas of practice where social workers often find themselves being challenged and having to challenge because of the cultures of expertise and power that can exist.

Standing up for service users' rights and welfare can be difficult in these arenas and action learning can support social workers in taking action in situations of adversity to create change, redress power and facilitate their own and others' learning.

Collaboration in context

Already asserted in this chapter is the notion that collaboration is viewed as a 'good thing' for social workers to be doing. It is viewed as a vital element to improving outcomes for service users, carers and families. In England, both the previous National Occupational Standards for Social Work (2002: 2) and current Professional Capabilities Framework highlight the requirement for social workers to *work effectively with others to improve services offered to individuals, families, carers, groups and communities.* Literature points towards some of the potential benefits of collaboration (Cheminais, 2009: 26):

- leads to enhanced and improved outcomes for children and young people, through a range of joined-up services, advice and support being readily available and easily accessible;

- helps to build consensus, strengthen partnership voice and break down professional boundaries and parochial attitudes;

- can help to build a more cohesive community approach through united multi-agency practitioners taking greater ownership and responsibility for addressing local needs jointly, thus avoiding duplication or overlap of provision;

- increased level of trust existing between partners/providers in relation to every-one knowing each can and will deliver;

- increased staff morale knowing that they do not work in isolation and that issues and problems can be resolved collaboratively;

- more enthusiastic and committed staff who have high expectations of them-selves and others.

The context for collaboration is an important one. Social work activity does not take place in isolation and every context is different; whether you are working in a child protection case conference or a multi-disciplinary team assessing for NHS continuing healthcare funding, each situation has different nuances and varia-bles. Differences might include the service user group, power dynamics between individuals because of different types of power (see Chapter 5) and personality types, types of professionals who have different qualifications, and so on. These scenarios are also distinctive because they occur at a unique space in time, each with its own political, economic and social dimension influencing the dynamic of the group. Furthermore, all professionals will have their own uniqueness and belief systems, including their family culture, education, emotional regulation (or dysregulation), and so forth. Therefore, collaboration is not quite as straightfor-ward as the law, policy and guidance tell us.

One challenging area in adult social work practice takes place in hospitals. In England, one of the most significant challenges for partnership practice was the introduction of the Community Care Act (Delayed Discharges) 2003. The announcement from central government for 'cross-charging' between health and social care was primarily aimed at improving the timely discharge of patients from hospital and effectively fining social service departments if they were found to cause delay in the assessment, care planning and provision of services. At the time, the Health Select Committee announced some support for cross-charging arrangements but also criticised such arrangements, stating:

> The proposals constituted a blunt instrument that, rather than improving partnership, would be likely to reinforce a negative blame culture.

> (House of Commons Select Committee, 2002, para. 162)

This was further reinforced by the Association of Directors of Social Services who commented that *such an arrangement would undermine trust and cooperation between health and social services* (ADSS, 2002). Moreover, the policy was thought to be an *ill-thought-through announcement that cast local authority social service departments as the villain of the piece* (Henwood, 2004: 401). However, despite the pessimism, the scale of delays did reduce and so there is a question of whether legislation directly impacted on this problem. Arguably, the numbers of delays were already in decline and the Commission for Social Care Inspection (2004: 4) noted, *behind these encouraging statistics lies a much more mixed picture, in terms of the quality of the person's experience.*

Building trust and cultures of co-operation is as important with each other and with other professions as it is with service users. Cultures which have high degrees of blame are unlikely to take responsibility for action, instead arguing that it was the fault of the doctor, the social worker or the occupational therapist. It is difficult to remove ourselves from such cultures when enshrined in statutory legislation is the requirement to find out who caused the delay or maybe, more aptly put: who's to blame here? The culture of blame and mistrust has been further seen in other critical areas of social work practice, including child protection. The death of Victoria Climbié in particular highlighted that multiple health and social work professionals had been involved in seeing and examining Victoria and assumptions were made about whose responsibility it was to follow up on certain actions – unfortunately with horrific consequences.

Whilst it is not our intention to go in depth into the legislation and policies related to multi-agency practice to protect children, it is important to recognise that this is not new ground. *Working Together to Safeguard Children* (Department of Health, 1991), for example, highlighted the requirement for a coordinated response from professionals to meet the needs of children who are suffering or likely to suffer from significant harm (Horwarth, 2001: 28). After the death of Victoria Climbié, the Children Act 2004 came into force, with statutory provision requiring local co-operation between local authorities, key partner agencies and other relevant bodies (Brayne and Carr, 2012). This duty to co-operate, it is argued, whilst giving the statutory provision, does not wholly address the issues of co-operating, collaborating or addressing the needs of children in a multi-agency context. The well-documented and sad death of Baby Peter Connelly in 2007 (also known as 'Baby P') arguably demonstrates that, despite the legislative reform and duty to co-operate, failings across health, social care and other relevant agencies to make appropriate decisions relevant to the safety and wellbeing of children will continue to be a challenge. As with Victoria Climbié, there had been multiple visits from health, social work and police; in Baby Peter Connelly's case, this amounted to 60 contacts over an eight-month period. The purpose of highlighting these two well-known and documented cases of child abuse is not to criticise but to demonstrate the challenge and difficulty in protecting children in contexts of change, uncertainty and stress.

There are similar stories in adult safeguarding where Serious Case Reviews have highlighted a number of 'lessons learned', particularly in the context of interagency practice. Manthorpe and Martineau's analysis of Serious Case Reviews in England identified:

> *the majority of the reports identified deficits in interagency communication, the exact nature of the deficit depending, of course, on the circumstances. These reports isolate the poor relationship between, for example, care staff (#8) or police (#8) or general practitioners*

(family doctors) or the hospital staff (#9) and the apparatus of adult safeguarding within the local authority.

(Manthorpe and Martineau, 2011: 234)

This study appears to mirror the picture across children services where neglect and abuse were not communicated or picked up by the respective authorities and where the interagency arrangements were not robust enough. Critically, the 'lessons learnt' from these types of inquiries into the deaths of vulnerable children or adults continue to expose interagency communication as one of the major practice deficits. However, the policies and legislation that offer guidance and procedures to be followed on collaborative practice have not appeared to eliminate the problem. Before looking into the practical application of action learning to support multi-agency practice, let us take a look at some of the challenges and opportunities to collaborate.

REFLECTION POINT

- *What are your experiences of working with other professionals?*

- *How does it feel to work with other professional groups, e.g. doctors, occupational therapists?*

- *Who had the most power and who had the least?*

- *What do you think are the key drivers that increase or decrease power between professionals?*

Challenges and opportunities for collaboration

Cheminais (2009: 26) offers a view on some of the challenges that collaboration brings across the multi-agency interface:

- lack of clarity over roles and responsibilities can lead to a blame culture and poor performance;

- competing organisational priorities, policies and procedures;

- the management of different cultures;

- language and protocol understanding;

- territorial issues, including sharing equipment and property;

- preventing too much 'passing the buck' to give the illusion of effective action being taken.

- *What multi-agency teams or groups have you been part of recently or in the past?*

- *Did they appear to work well?*

- *What were the main advantages to working in this way?*

- *Were there challenges that did not easily resolve themselves, maybe because of a strong personality in the group or power held by a particular profession?*

- *How did you feel as a social worker/social work student being part of a group of multi-professionals?*

It appears that there are a number of opportunities and challenges for multi-agency practice in social work. Arguably, the increased challenges that a multi-agency group faces are the wide cultural and professional differences, compared with groups of social workers or nurses who work together. In action learning, however, we would argue there are clear opportunities with having a range of different professions, so diversity can bring understanding about these very differences and similarities of culture and profession. Despite our optimism for multi-agency practice, it must be recognised that a number of different factors are involved in successful action learning sets in order to bring about change, outcomes and processes that facilitate action and learning. The challenge and opportunity that action learning can bring to multi-agency practice include:

- an ethical and value-based methodology, which clearly links with social work values, for looking at real-time problems with your colleagues to understand the issues, problems and opportunities;

- action is a core tenet of action learning sets where real problem solving can be addressed and taken away from the set, ready to be reviewed for the next time;

- the thinking, feeling and willing elements of questioning help different professionals engage at different levels of the problem rather than simply focusing on one area, e.g. action or thinking;

- emotional engagement of the issue is more likely to elicit underlying assumptions about the challenge and a step away from technical/rational solutions that arguably achieve very little long-term change;

- a variety of different methods to use for different multi-agency issues, e.g. five-step model, constellations;

- time and space offered to reflect on action and, importantly, to explore critically the power, politics, context and assumptions of the problem at hand;

- allows you to become aware of your social position, role and identity in a group and how this fits into the wider cultural and societal expectations of you as a person and as a social work practitioner.

ACTIVITY **6.1**

Explore how action learning can be used in your practice with other multi-agency professionals. For example, if you are working in a hospital environment, you might consider questioning whether more could be done in multi-professional team meetings on your ward. How could action learning sets realistically work in your environment? Would they add value to solving the 'wicked' problems? Further considerations will include 'buy-in' from others (particularly 'expert' consultants), time, number of people, ground rules and the understanding of all set members of how action learning sets 'work' (or don't!).

Professional identity

Social workers can offer a lot to multi-agency groups, teams or organisations. As we explored in Chapter 4, emotionally and socially engaged practitioners are far more likely to create environments where lateral thinking, harmony and optimism are commonplace. In the multi-agency context, practice which is overly focused on the task without considering other influences, such as emotion, power and assumptions, is arguably in trouble. Learning is likely to be impaired when subtle nuances or overt influences are ignored. In action learning, social workers can play a role in a multi-agency context by asking questions that offer challenging insights to other professions. Each profession has its own codes of practice and ways of doing things, at times, to the detriment of service users. Social workers therefore have a role to play and an identity in promoting social justice, exploring emotional wellbeing and facing up to the social and political influences in times of adversity.

The social worker identity has arguably altered over the years. A move away from relationship-based social work towards case management in the 1990s has seen managerialism, procedures and bureaucraticism become the social work *raison d'être*. Howe quotes Gorman regarding this shift towards case management:

> *I don't have time to sit and talk with the person I am assessing for services. Care management has altered professional identity so that the therapeutic element and the skills one considered to be integral to [social work] practice barely apply. Brokerage, accountancy and political manoeuvring are far more relevant.*

(Howe, 2008: 193)

Gorman gives a stark account of her social work practice and a critical examination of care management. Munro (2011: 10–12) has highlighted some of the deficits in multi-agency practice, which has too much prescription and procedure laid down for practitioners and organisations.

- Complying with prescription and keeping records to demonstrate compliance have become too dominant. The centrality of forming relationships with children and families to understand and help them has become obscured.

- The review has concluded that the high levels of prescription have also hampered the profession's ability to take responsibility for developing its own knowledge and skills.

- In moving to a system that promotes the exercise of professional judgement, local multi-agency systems will need to be better at monitoring, learning and adapting their practice.

- The priority given to process over practice has led to insufficient attention being given to whether children and young people are benefiting from the services they receive.

We would agree with Munro's view that any system needs to continue to adapt to the pace of change around it and this goes back to Revans's equation $L \geq C$, or learning must be greater than or equal to the rate of external change for survival. Social workers must therefore reflect on their role identity and where they can fit into a multi-agency context as we argue that they have a significant role to play in navigating through the myriad of policy, procedure and politics that encompasses health, social care, the police and education. The emphasis from Munro's report highlights the need to move back towards relationship-based social work and greater autonomy for professional decision making and away from procedures, cultures of managerialism and policies that overly prescribe.

Action learning can support the questioning of insight into procedures and policy and to problem solve. As a social worker, whether you're in a community team looking at prevention or in an acute hospital setting looking at safe and timely discharges, you have a vital part to play. In our experience, multi-agency groups are often chaired by a non-social work professional. Whether this is a consultant psychiatrist in a mental health meeting or a senior police officer in an adult safeguarding multi-agency meeting, social workers rarely see themselves leading a multi-agency group. In action learning, the emphasis of a chair person or someone who is perceived to have more expertise is discouraged since you are all viewed as peers and *comrades in adversity* who are there to question, support and take action on challenges and problems. This is helpful because it takes away the hierarchy and 'expert' position of some set members who are there to give advice, solve everyone's problems for them and take away any chance of learning from the group. As we have already seen, Revans was interested in what people did not know rather than what they did. In multi-agency contexts there may be greater competition from those wishing to 'treat' the problem rather than wanting to question the insight into the problem so as to support the individual in taking action and then learning through reflection on action.

- *What does it mean to you to be a professional social worker (or if you're a social work student, what will it mean)?*

- *What do you think the power relations are like with your health/education/ police/other colleagues?*

- *Do you feel that you are valued as a multi-agency member? In what way?*

- *How do you value the identity of being a social worker?*

- *What actions can you take or have you taken to uphold the social work identity?*

Decision making in groups

Most decisions are made with some level of consultation with others, whether in our personal or professional lives. As we have seen in Chapter 2, decision making is a key area of practice for social workers, from referral through to making decisions about closing or banking cases for review. However, some decisions can be made without lots of consultation because they are critical problems, requiring little collaboration from others, having little uncertainty and being resolvable through unlinear actions (Grint, 2005). Johnson and Williams (2007: 102) argue that, at times, it must be acknowledged that decisions cannot achieve the optimal results in problem solving because of the limited choice available to front-line practitioners mainly due to the economic constraints of care provision. We have also critically visited the notion of decision making in a context of emotions and power, which has been argued as commonplace in the world of social work practice. Thus, decision making is not easy and at times requires judgements to be made in situations which have consequences for service users' lives and their carers. Social workers inherently can have a lot of power, responsibility and accountability in relation to the decisions they make. Here are some of the areas where social workers come face to face with difficult ethical dilemmas and where decisions can have consequences for the organisation they work for, the service users, their carers and themselves:

- decisions relating to child protection proceedings;

- recommendations for adoption;

- care planning and commissioning arrangements with service users and carers;

- referral decisions to investigate under child protection/adult safeguarding procedures;

- recommendations for NHS continuing healthcare;
- mental health tribunals;
- youth offending panel decisions;
- assessment and reviews.

Action learning sets are much more helpful for 'wicked problems' than tame or critical problems since the latter two types of problem require less collaboration. The power in action learning comes from the wider perspectives and questions that challenge insight and assumptions for the problem holder so new actions can be formulated and taken out of the set into the real world. There are thus choices to be made and decisions to be taken regarding action. It is also argued that there are choices in how the problem holder views the issue, which is influenced by the context and the individual's motivation, emotion and patterns of thinking into action. Our experiences of decision making in social work appear to be more frequently taken 'on the hoof' without full regard to how that decision is made and with little real critical analysis. We argue that for decisions to be made which are 'wicked' in nature, the set members can offer clarity to the problem and support action which has had the thinking, feeling and willing exposed in a social setting (the set) rather than simply being contained within the problem holder. The set can function as a thermostatic control and can ask questions which test the temperature of the action. If it's a decision that is going to cause people to get into hot water, then the questions can reflect how the set member feels about the ethical nature or consequences to others and society.

Ethical decision making and action appear to have been at the heart of Reg Revans's *raison d'être*. Revans was interested in real problem solving, not artificial or fabricated problems, and lived a life based on many of the fundamental principles of social work, often giving up his time for free or for very little money. According to Boshyk and Dilworth:

> *He lived a Spartan existence, eating sparingly. It was discovered years after he had worked in Belgium, gaining a pension entitlement, that he had never claimed it. His interest was in making the world a better place and promoting the kind of dialogue that could advance understanding.*

> (Boshyk and Dilworth, 2010: 29)

Decision making and choices which make the world a better place are welcomed for social workers who are actively and genuinely engaged in emancipatory practice and who are willing to act as agents of change in a context of oppression and discrimination. Choices for social workers in many organisations can be limited because of funding restrictions, particularly in austere times, and where there is a culture of risk aversion and high degrees of managerialism and for those who are under the spell of 'expert instruction'. However, we suggest that the power of action learning can be harnessed into action which can become genuinely empowering and question insight into complex ethical issues where supervision and other forms of support are not available or allowed in teams and organisations. Some of the more difficult decisions social workers have to make must be worked on within legal frameworks, guidance and statutory legislation. This can be helpful but also restrict social work practice because it often only allows for prescriptive practice. As we saw in Chapter 3, decision making in the Mental Capacity Act 2005 area does not necessarily allow for emotions to be seen in the context of decision making; instead it asks for social workers and health professionals to provide rational decisions based on cool and rational (or not) responses from service users. There are similar situations across children and adult social work practice where 'wicked problems' are attempted to be resolved by critical and tame problem-solving methods or by 'experts'.

> REFLECTION POINT
>
> - *What decisions do you need to make with service users, in your team and in your organisation?*
> - *How do you normally go about taking action on a situation?*
> - *Do you have enough time to make ethical decisions and, if so, how is this achieved?*
> - *How does your organisation promote decision making that is in line with social work ethics and values? Are there any areas of conflict?*

Groups can work extremely well and there are clear benefits for sets that have committed members willing to give equal measures of challenge and support. However the opposite can be true where there is too much willingness to comply and get on with one another, avoiding any hint of criticality and to the detriment of the decision-making process. Janis (1972) used the term *groupthink* to identify teams and groups that become fixed in states of blaming others outside the group or conforming to an agreed consensus (Gray *et al.*, 2010: 111). Arguably, this process can be exacerbated further in multi-agency groups where a dominant chair person can lead the group into unquestioned practices because of his or her domineering approach and where group members are too frightened to challenge decisions made. Set members and facilitators need to be acutely aware of this phenomenon, particularly where there is a strong leader, high group cohesion and lots of pressure from the outside to make a good decision (Janis, 1972).

The Pearl Harbor attack in 1941 is one high-profile case where the likelihood of an attack by Japanese fighters was rationalised and subsequently the perceived threat was deeply minimised. Although this is an extreme case and one which had many fatal consequences, it is a stark lesson on how groups can behave. The social work task is steeped in high degrees of uncertainty when it comes to ethical decision making and the action learning set will have a challenging time to reflect critically, explore and take action on choices with other practitioners, who may have very different perspectives on the problem.

CASE STUDY 6.1

'I thought they were supposed to be doing that'

In the Golden Jubilee of Action Learning Revans (1988) comments on the dire situation of 1987 when a number of children were taken away from their parents in Middlesborough, because of the risk of sexual abuse they were thought to have suffered. A total of 121 cases of suspected child abuse were diagnosed by two paediatricians and many children were removed from their parents' care. The subsequent judgement in the courts identified that 96 of the 121 cases were to be dismissed and 26 children from 12 families were found by judges to be incorrectly diagnosed.

Corby (2000: 43–44) highlights a number of reasons which contributed towards the rash decision to remove children from the care of their parents:

- *heightened awareness of the possible extent of child sexual abuse amongst social services and community paediatricians;*

- *the paediatricians were convinced about the validity of the reflex anal dilation test and their determination to use it;*

- *other agencies, including the police, who were more traditional in their approach and did not accept the findings created an interprofessional split.*

Following the Beckford Inquiry, the social services department had recently reorganised itself.

The subsequent Butler-Sloss (1988) report identified how coordination between the services intended to look after the children of Cleveland was almost completely lacking, and social workers, paediatricians, the police, parents and school teachers were not seldom in conflict rather than in harmony. Revans (1988: 26) notes that the report identified that: It is unacceptable that the disagreements and failure of communication of adults should be allowed to obscure the needs of children. *The Daily Telegraph stated:*

> It paints a vivid, despairing picture of professionals squabbling like fighting cocks, each jealously guarding old territory or building new empires while, behind them in the background, bewildered children and devastated adults are crowded into courts and hospital wards and foster homes, powerless victims of impersonal crusading zeal.

The Cleveland case identified how professionals had not worked together on the serious issue of sexual abuse and had overzealously removed a number of children from parents without establishing the social situation and solely using medical evidence. The effect of this case resulted in the Working Together

> *guidance and impacted on the implementation of the Children Act 1989, with a number of hasty amendments taking place before going through parliament (Corby, 2000). Revans (1988: 27) argues:*
>
> > What will certainly surprise such pioneers, such anticipators of confusions like that of Cleveland, such observers of social and economic reality as know from first-hand experience the competitive jealousies of experts with letters after their name, will be any action taken on the Butler-Sloss Report that, in any way whatsoever, pays attention to what George Wieland had to say about the approach of action learning to help hospitals of London.

It appears that Revans had a lot to say about the collaboration required between professionals in order to make difficult decisions regarding child protection cases. Action learning between different professionals may have supported a different outcome to this situation, although it appears the medical dominance, as seen earlier, may have overridden any sense of challenge to this professional and 'expert' culture. As social workers, you will have to make difficult decisions yourself with others and the balance between challenging others and not entering a *groupthink* situation will determine what actions and outcomes will be achieved for vulnerable adults and children. Becoming critically reflective in action learning sets and questioning assumptions and power will support the necessary actions to be taken outside the set and for decisions to be taken with your *comrades in adversity*.

Chapter summary

- Multi-agency practice is not straightforward or easy and at times is unsatisfactory. Instances of child and adult deaths, abuse and neglect have not been picked up where there have been insufficient ways of dealing with concerns, particularly in relation to communication.

- There has been much policy and even primary legislation towards improving partnership practice, although the reality is somewhat different from the rhetoric.

- Challenges and opportunities exist for professionals involved in multi-agency practice and action learning has been highlighted as a practical and pragmatic methodology in real-time multi-professional problem solving.

- Social workers have an important role to play in multi-agency groups, including in multi-professional action learning sets, to challenge the views held by other practitioners, which may be at odds with emancipation, social work values and social justice.

- The social work role and identity in multi-agency settings can be a difficult one to define and requires individuals and organisations to recognise the unique skills, knowledge and challenge social workers bring to some of the most difficult and challenging issues.

- Action learning provides a pragmatic methodology which can help real-time problem solving for multi-professionals ready to take action (and learn).

- Critically, the culture of the organisation, team or multi-agency is an important factor in whether multi-agency practice is effective or not; action learning sets can provide the bedrock to develop capacities for thinking, feeling and willing.

- Decision making in groups, including the interdisciplinary context, is challenging and steeped in ethical dilemmas; action learning can support ethical decision making through reflection on the thinking, feeling and willing elements of the human action and weighing up the consequences to actions before they are taken in real time.

FURTHER READING

Johnson, K. and Williams, I. (2007) *Managing Uncertainty and Change in Social Work and Social Care.* Lyme Regis: Russell House Publishing.

Lymbery, M. (2006) United we stand? Partnership working in health and social care and the role of social work in services for older people. *British Social Work Journal,* 36: 1119–1134.

Quinney, A. (2006) *Collaborative Social Work Practice.* Exeter: Learning Matters.

Chapter 7

Case studies: action learning sets in action

We have brought together four case studies for you to read and reflect upon. We have chosen to do this in order to integrate fully into practice the realities of action learning sets working at different structural levels. The case studies include one focusing mainly on the individual set member experience as well as a case study on multi-organisational practice. After each case study there are questions which allow you to reflect upon each of the scenarios and whether they struck a chord with you, how you felt about the situation and what actions you might have taken. Decision making in sets is explored in these case studies, reflecting the nature of action learning and the requirement in social work to take action on challenges faced daily by social workers caught up with 'wicked problems'.

We hope that some of the earlier theory and principles of action learning become further contextualised from Parts 1 and 2. There are some reflection points throughout the chapter for you to explore and reflect on your own practice.

CASE STUDY 7.1

The individual in a set: the power of action learning

An action learning set was established by a local authority in England for social workers who were part of a newly qualified programme to support their practice as qualified practitioners and enhance their problem-solving skills. The group

---

comprised six newly qualified social workers (NQSWs) who worked across adult and children services in three different authorities. The set had a ratio of five females to one male and there was a mix of ethnic backgrounds. Initially the action learning set explored ground rules which included confidentiality (and its limits), timeliness and punctuality, high challenge and support, how the actions were to be recorded and a commitment to fulfilling those actions. The set met a total of eight times over the course of ten months and was facilitated by an experienced social work practitioner.

Initially the action learning set was very reluctant to engage in coming up with a problem or issue that affected them in the workplace. It took several sessions to engage them in even describing some of the problems they were facing with service users, their peers and work colleagues. A further struggle for the set was realising the difference between a tame problem and a 'wicked problem' and the set members wanting to solve 'puzzles'. On two occasions a set member brought someone else's problem and fabricated another. Avoidance of real problems and issues which resulted in them feeling stuck became commonplace until one set member, Sally, took a leap of faith in disclosing an issue she had with her team manager.

Sally worked in a children's team and spoke about how she felt about the team manager, who was described as having no organisational skills and where allocations 'are handed out like sweets'. Other emotional experiences were explored, including the feeling that when the team manager was nearby, Sally felt like her heart was racing and her stomach was turning inside itself. Sally explained to the set that she felt angry about not being listened to and that the expectations of her were too high. She identified that she had a very good relationship with her supervisor John but he was also struggling to work with the team manager. It was clearly a problem which had no right or wrong answer and some action would certainly help Sally to feel better about the situation. Using the five-step method the set asked a number of questions to define the problem and explore the context and power relationships between Sally and her team manager.

The perceived quality of relationships between the team manager and a number of other team members was also explored in more depth as well as how Sally felt she fitted into the team. A lot of anger and frustration was described by Sally and it was clear that she had come to breaking point with the team manager. This was interesting because she had not voiced any concern in the previous two sets, despite her feeling exceptionally stuck in this problem, which was affecting how she thought about the team, organisation and service users. Sally explored that it was no longer pressure but she was feeling stressed out by her team manager who had the responsibility for ensuring her caseload was protected and that allocations were appropriate to her level of capability. Because her feelings appeared to be overwhelming and overriding any sense of calm and reasoned thinking, the facilitator modelled questions about her previous actions and successes in the team and also asked questions which provoked more 'objective' rational thinking.

This appeared to help separate the tide of emotion which was causing a lot of the feelings of being stuck. The thinking questions about what actions the team manager had previously taken and what Sally thought about the situation rather than what she felt helped create some new perspectives of thinking. In doing so, Sally looked calmer and more relaxed in how she answered questions. Sally stated that she thought that the team manager did not have enough time herself to manage the workload and that she was 'running around like a headless chicken most of the time'. Despite Sally recognising the behaviours of her manager, which were mostly unhelpful from her perspective, she realised that she had also been reacting to how the manager was behaving and probably feeling, by becoming stressed, with her heart racing and her stomach turning. Sally had felt that it was her responsibility to pick up cases even though she knew that she would be stressed about additional casework. Sally began to realise that it was her own thinking processes and her behaviour that caused her to become stressed and that she had not told the manager how she genuinely felt. With the support of the set, some actions were explored and written down for her to do before the next meeting:

- Sally to raise the issue of feeling stressed and anxious about her caseload in her next supervision and for this to be recorded;

- arrange a three-way meeting with her supervisor and manager to discuss the expectations of casework and how she felt about her situation;

- behave in a more assertive manner at the next allocation meeting about what she can realistically take and what she cannot.

The set worked well on this issue and asked questions that challenged Sally's insight into the problem and some of her assumptions. For example, Sally had never spoken to the team manager about how she felt and this was partly due to her dislike of some of the manager's behaviours but also because she did not feel confident in saying 'no'. Sally realised that there were power differences between herself as a newly qualified practitioner and her manager and yet there was a need to take a calculated risk in discussing this with her directly, albeit with the support from her supervisor.

At the next action learning set, Sally reviewed her actions with the group who were excited about listening to what had happened. Sally explained that she had met with her team manager with the support of her supervisor and had a very honest conversation about how she was feeling. Sally said that this was *very hard as emotions and feelings rarely get spoken about in her team and that she felt 'emotionally exposed'. However, despite the initial anxiety, her manager responded positively to her and thanked her for her candid view. It transpired that no one had spoken to her about how they were feeling in the team so she had assumed that practitioners were taking on cases because they were able to. At the next allocation meeting, Sally stated that she felt 'more liberated' and confident to say what she was able to take and what she could not. In the six weeks between the two action learning sets, her relationship with her team manager had improved vastly and there was a 'felt shift' in her approach to social work, not just in the context of allocations but more widely with her work with service users.*

Sally reviewed her decision making and the learning that had taken place at the fourth action learning set and concluded that the original problem that she was facing was not the team manager but actually her own perspective on the issue and how emotionally the situation had become overwhelming. As a result, her work suffered and she dreaded coming into work, especially on a Monday when allocations were distributed in the team. Sally had also raised the issue in supervision that, whilst she had a good relationship with her supervisor, it was not helping her to become emotionally resilient and problem solving was always based on puzzles and caseload management rather than exploring other issues that were affecting her practice. Sally also commented on how the support of the set had enabled her to become increasingly confident and to challenge current allocation practices with the team manager, despite at first feeling somewhat anxious at this prospect. Interestingly, when Sally took the leap of faith with the set and made the decision to explore the problem, the rest of the set became a lot less anxious about bringing problems and challenges they faced, almost as if permission had been given for problem solving in the set.

- *Could you relate to any parts of this problem and, if so, how?*
- *What were the areas that you could identify with?*
- *How did you feel when you read Sally's issue?*
- *Can you see any skills being developed by Sally and her comrades in adversity and, if so, what were they?*
- *What actions would you have taken in Sally's situation?*

CASE STUDY **7.2**

Transformation programme: a multi-agency approach

The Linthorpe transformation programme was created to improve health and social care services in the county. Health, local authorities and emergency services were invited to take part in a number of projects, called the Linthorpe transformation programme, to improve health and social care outcomes in the county. As part of the project, three action learning sets were established from 22 volunteer professionals. This case study concerns one of the sets. Members of the set represented the ambulance service, hospital trust, local authority social services, local authority housing department, general practice and community health services. John, a paramedic, Jeff, a housing officer, Lucy, a senior nurse, Jane, a senior social worker, Mohammed, a GP, Len, a community physiotherapist and Amena, a consultant physician formed the set. One of the problems that the set addressed was the care of a stroke patient from the first call to the ambulance service to discharge from hospital and rehabilitation at home. All the set members were interested in this issue in that they knew that the service they and their agencies provided to patients/clients was inadequate but were at a loss as to what was wrong let alone how to address the issues.

At the beginning there were, in the set, disparities in perceived power. During the meetings, this manifested itself in different ways. At first, the paramedic and housing officer reported that they felt intimidated by the others, particularly the medical staff, and didn't feel they could contribute to the problem. The social worker said she felt isolated and the group was hostile to her profession. The nurse had been a student on the ward where the medical consultant was the senior consultant and said she felt nervous in conversation with her. The physiotherapist and GP worked together in the community and came to and from the meetings together, often sharing stories of both work and the village cricket team that they both played for.

At the first few meetings, everyone was polite and respectful but no action was taken. The set looked as though it would disband, as many were feeling despondent.

At the third meeting, this changed. Two days earlier John, the paramedic, had received an emergency call to attend a patient who had had a stroke; when he got to the nearest hospital Amena was the consultant on emergency duty. They started to discuss the initial care of the patient at home and John talked about how inadequate he felt. Amena talked about the importance of this first response to the situation and that John's role was vital. Amena also talked about the care in the emergency department and how she often felt angry that the stroke patient was left when more immediately life-threatening cases came in. At the set meeting Amena volunteered to go out with the ambulance crew and John in turn volunteered to spend time with Amena in the stroke clinic. This

CASE STUDY 7.2 continued

led to others in the set looking at other handover points – from nurse to social worker, consultant to physiotherapist and GP and social worker to housing officer.

Each agreed to shadow each other and report back the results to the set before the next meeting. Everyone kept a diary of their visit and this was shared together with the outstanding questions and what was learned through the process. All agreed that by 'walking in each other's shoes', they gained a better understanding of both each other's roles and the conditions and pressures each worked under. In particular, Jane and Lucy were surprised that, consciously putting aside the professional and organisational tensions, they could find ways of supporting each other, particularly in the administration processes. Lucy recalled: 'I confess that, before, just seeing that a social worker would be involved with a patient filled me with despair – more paperwork, meetings, and for what? All I could see was people more concerned with their budget than the patient.' Jane too revealed her perception of the medical and nursing teams colluding and 'hiding behind a medical model of care'. Mohammed summed up: 'In the set we were all encouraged to openly talk about these barriers between professions. It was awkward at first but we ended up laughing at each other's perceptions of us and recognised them as being caricatures, not real people.'

One of the actions from shadowing each other was the recognition that the voice of the patient/client was not being heard. It was agreed that John, the paramedic, and Jeff, the housing officer, would meet with the local stroke association and Lucy, Jane, Mohammed and Amena would talk to patients and clients.

John reported how good it was to talk with people other than in a crisis situation and see the outcomes of some of those he had taken to hospital. Jeff also went to visit some of the stroke association members in their own homes to see the practical solutions in terms of housing adaptations.

Shadowing the social worker helped Jeff see the urgency of the requests that came from the social work team and Jane recognised the importance of the questions that were asked by the housing team that often seemed irrelevant.

Lucy, Amena, Jane, Mohammed and Len all declared that they had in the past conducted satisfaction surveys about the services they offered but recognised this focused on the 'what we do as individual services, not the whole journey'. So they agreed a survey format that focused on the transfer from one service to another, and the quality of that rather than individual service interventions. 'We all had good services and nobody doubted that, but we were all surprised at the patients'/clients' stories of the journey. Some reported getting lost in the system – gaps in care – inequality of services, and importantly, many said they recognised that the different professions either just 'didn't have respect for each other' or 'openly fought against each other.'

There were a number of practical projects that came out of this first stage and were handed on to teams to plan and organise. Outcomes of this investigative phase were to:

1. provide information to shops and restaurants about recognising the symptoms of strokes and what to do;

2. consider other emergency professions, particularly police and prison officers, as some people presenting with stroke symptoms may appear to be drunk, drug abusers or violent;

3. provide additional training for the emergency teams in both the ambulance services and accident and emergency departments.

One of the most striking outcomes for the set was the recognition of how little they helped each other and indeed were helped. The major issue was the communication between agencies in the way they organise services and the professions. In fact, even more, when difficulties occurred they all believed that they were under attack and therefore they felt under an obligation to defend their profession or agency. In addition, all recognised that in a concerted attempt to do their job correctly they failed to focus on the whole journey for the patient/client.

REFLECTION POINT

- Could you relate to any parts of this problem and if so, how?

- What were the areas that you could identify with?

- How did you feel when you read Jane's part in the process?

- Can you see any skills being developed by Jane and her comrades in adversity and if so, what were they?

- What actions would you have taken in Jane's situation?

CASE STUDY 7.3

Action learning in teams: a way of working

The Feldwith Social Services Directorate had employed six NQSWs and had decided to use action learning as a way of supporting them through the first year of their practice. Jo was employed in the Adult Care Team and was asked to join the action learning set by the practice educator.

It started when I was an NQSW in my first year in practice. I was a mature student and my new manager is 20 years younger than me. During a supervision session, he told me that I would be joining an action learning set to support me in my practice. It was a new scheme in the authority; in fact, it was new to social care. I was surprised it was so new. I had worked in a hospital as a health care assistant and there action learning had been around for some time. In fact I was part of a set that included nurses, occupational therapists and doctors.

Jo felt the set would have benefited from a mix of experience rather than just all newly qualified staff but the practice educator was not convinced, so she went to her manager describing her experience in the NHS. Steve listened; he too had previously worked in a hospital social work team and, although he had not taken part in an action learning set, he had seen service improvement take place in multi-professional teams using action learning principles. Having looked at the Skills for Care website for more information, Steve found there was an opportunity to go on an introduction to action learning programme for managers with NQSWs in their team:

I felt like I had come home; the principles of action learning, the support and challenge in groups and the opportunity to look more critically and creatively to look at social work problems seemed to me to match the values of social work.

I knew that many of my staff who were new to social work had only experienced care management as a way of working and the more experienced staff were hardened and cynical so I felt this was an opportunity to try something new to improve the service we offer our clients and the motivation of the team.

Jo said she was somewhat relieved that Steve was enthusiastic and together they planned to introduce action learning to the team. Steve decided that it would need to be introduced slowly. 'I knew that there would be some cynics and that if this was going to work we needed enthusiastic volunteers.' He and Jo together did a short presentation to six other members of the team and demonstrated an action learning set with Jo presenting a problem. Volunteers were sought and two out of the six present came forward, with Jo and Steve, who made up half of the team.

The set met every two weeks and looked at a case that someone was working on that was interesting but where there were outstanding questions. The manager, Steve, recalled:

At first the set found it hard to not go straight to the solutions and particularly for Jo we all wanted to go to advice giving. It was difficult not to want to give her the benefit of our 'wisdom'. One of the set said that she found it hard not to try to prove she had the answers.

Steve got in touch with the person who ran the programme he attended to talk about how the set could move on. 'I do think that was a turning point and for anyone wanting to do this, I would encourage them to find a network to support them through the early stages of this way of working.' Steve was put in touch with other people from introductory programmes and the set they had formed to support managers introducing action learning.

'Out of that I suggested that we practised asking questions focusing on the issue presented, using the thinking, feeling and willing model.' Jo brought a lemon to the set and anybody giving advice was presented with the lemon. 'It caused great amusement and people actually picked the lemon up themselves as a reminder when they felt themselves about to give advice or solutions! . . . It felt strange at first but gradually we did start to trust each and talk about our anxieties as well as just the technical stuff.' The support and camaraderie became evident to the rest of the team and this encouraged others to join and eventually the whole team joined. Jo acknowledged: 'It was difficult at first; we had to demonstrate the process to the others, but we soon got the hang of it.'

The set started to work on becoming more critical in the questioning, testing each other's assumptions and the politics of the cases they were working on.

The team felt it was improving the decision making both individually and as a team.

> We looked at cases more critically in terms of why we were acting in the way we were. The way we did supervision was different as well. It has become much more work load management – it always was, to be honest, but now we are open about that and the team professionally peer supervise the cases.

> I felt I was being supported by the whole team, not just Steve. Knowing that other more experienced members of the team also struggled with some of the decisions they were making was strangely comforting. It helps me be more grounded in my practice.

The team agreed that they were all learning from and with each other and felt this was therefore more than just case work.

Other teams in the authority have also noticed the way that Steve's team works. The team are openly supportive of each other but not in a way that they collude

---

CASE STUDY *7.3 continued*

with each other; stress levels are lower and staff seem to have time to develop themselves professionally. Recently they have taken part in a national research project, for example.

Other social workers in the authority asked about the success of Steve's team. 'I guess we have been quite secretive about what we were doing, not because we wanted it to be a secret, but because we felt fragile until we had established this way of working robustly.' The support of the action learning set Steve was in outside the organisation helped the set maintain a distance from the organisation and helped Steve's own confidence.

REFLECTION POINT

- Could you relate to any parts of this case and if so, how?

- What were the areas that you could identify with?

- What actions would you have taken in Steve's position when Jo suggested action learning in the team?

- How did you feel when you read how Jo and Steve worked together?

- Can you see any skills being developed by this team and if so, what were they?

CASE STUDY *7.4*

An organisational programme: challenges and opportunities

NQSWs (in adult services) have been supported for the last few years by Skills for Care and have invested to develop action learning facilitator programmes. Social work as a profession has recognised the importance of developing the skills and values and of consolidating knowledge at the NQSW level and the use of action learning sets has supported newly qualified practitioners across England. A local authority in northern England nominated an experienced social worker, Susan, to take part in a four-day facilitator programme and subsequently the Institute of Leadership and Management level 5 certificate in facilitating action learning. Following the completion of each award, action learning became embedded in practice with NQSWs on the assessed and supported year of employment and also two other sets established with more experienced social workers and team managers to tackle challenges and opportunities.

Each set appeared dissatisfied with a number of areas related to their supervision, which was described as a 'tick box exercise', overly focused on performance management, and a culture of blame had set in across three teams that experienced a number of staff going off sick with stress and burnout, as well as a staff member experiencing disciplinary action. Rather than tackling issues which fundamentally affected them as social workers and real problem solving, there was deep resentment about some of the team managers and senior managers who were felt to be at the root of the problems. Several set members commented:

> I'm becoming disheartened with the whole process. I didn't get into social work to become a form filler, I thought I was going to make a change.

> My time with service users is less and less; I'm in the office more than ever now and I'm getting even more stuck with some of the problems.

> My supervision is awful – I get one hour a month which basically feels like an exercise in 'covering your backside'.

The action learning set with the more experienced social workers engaged with the methodology and understood the principles and purpose well. The set continues to this day and has a natural energy and motivation to support each other and critically reflect on their practice in a very candid and open way. High levels of trust and co-operation have helped the set raise organisational issues as well as challenges they faced with service users who were difficult to engage and other professionals and colleagues who they struggled to collaborate with.

Unfortunately, the team manager group struggled with getting to grips with the purpose and felt that it was not relevant to their role. One of the managers stated: 'I'm not sure how this action learning is really going to help; my team is working well already.' Some managers avoided the sets completely, which made it difficult to get a consistent and committed group of people together to tackle real issues. There appeared to be conflict and competition about the importance of one problem over another and poor trust amongst set members. The facilitator in this situation had attempted to start action learning as a set adviser without recognising the importance of asking the question: Is the organisation ready for action learning? The crucial role, advocated for by Reg Revans of the 'accoucheur' (or birth attendant) was not recognised and, instead of developing trust and cooperation, a dysfunctional set of behaviours led to the eventual abandonment of the set.

Despite this knockback, the organisation recognised the importance of action learning and a report was sent to the senior management team which was approved by the director. Organisationally, this appeared to be a step in the right direction and a glimmer of hope was seen by some as change was on the horizon (due to the austerity measures and a major restructure) and a new approach to tackling these changes was required. The local authority decided upon using a solution-focused model of change management and 'coaching' to overcome any barriers and challenges, rather than using action learning sets, and 'experts' continue to be widely used to tackle the complex tasks involved in change and team restructuring. Underneath the corporate lens, however, action learning sets continued for more experienced social workers and NQSWs who, despite the challenges detailed above, grew in strength as 'comrades in adversity' to support one another and ask fresh questions about what was really going on for them as social workers in a climate of uncertainty and a culture of blame and insecurity.

The facilitator, Susan, in her reflections highlighted some interesting points about the challenges and opportunities action learning had in her organisation. She wrote that the social workers who worked well and created high levels of energy were the ones who recognised the issues around them whilst she felt the team managers were avoidant and were not ready to challenge each other in the face of management cuts and an oppressive blame culture. In her feedback report, she identified that:

- I can see the real benefits of rolling this out across the teams and even across departments and organisations. The tricky bit is getting the organisation to believe and change old habits and see something with a fresh pair of eyes.

- It's a great idea, but when I was faced with so much pessimism, particularly from the team managers, it gave me little hope that they we were ready, or the organisation to embrace the change and get things done.

- I love facilitating the experienced social worker group; they have learnt so much, not just about themselves, but some of the things they took for granted in their practice and also about how they learnt. It was genuinely powerful – we've had so many 'Eureka' moments when one of us in the set has realised something about themselves that we didn't know before.

- For once I now have an opportunity to be part of something that is really making people take the time to think and challenge assumptions on practice. We've become really challenging and also even more supportive at the same time – the combination somehow works.

Susan had also noted that, despite the apparent sign-up by the senior management team, there was little cultural change in the service and so the social workers in the teams had experienced very little wisdom from

> *above, despite doubt ascending! Instead, doubt ascending was met by the maintenance of the organisational status quo and risk avoidance, keeping with experts (external project managers and consultants) who appeared to leave the organisation in the same position as before.*

REFLECTION POINT

- *What do you think the challenges and opportunities are in implementing action learning sets into organisations?*

- *What were the areas that you could identify with?*

- *How did you feel when you read Susan's reflections?*

- *What actions could you take to improve the motivation and uptake from social work managers?*

- *How much power do you think the organisation had in Susan's situation?*

Chapter summary

- There are a number of opportunities and challenges that action learning presents to individuals, teams and organisations.

- At the individual level, how we feel and how we transform our feelings into action are supported by sets with high challenge and high levels of support.

- Overwhelming emotions that are stressful appeared to be at the heart of the issue with Sally and the set helped her to reframe her perspective, take action and move forward in her relationship with her team manager.

- A multi-agency approach using action learning supported real-time problem solving, despite the action learning set not challenging each other enough at the beginning.

- Taking time to reflect on the patient journey rather than doing the job 'correctly' helped each set member view the problem in a different way, becoming less defensive in the process and striving to achieve a positive outcome for the service user.

- It may be difficult at times to resist the urge and temptation of going straight towards solutions. Avoiding this temptation and asking fresh questions appeared to create a team which supported and challenged one another – in the end becoming quite secretive about why they were so successful!

- It appears that some organisations are not ready or not willing to become 'learning organisations' and, even if they are, it requires a good 'midwife of learning' to kick-start the action required.

- However, even if the top layer of management cannot yet visualise how powerful action learning can be, social workers can still perform underneath the corporate radar to challenge oppressive practice, develop their emotional and social skills and become practitioners who are critical and, importantly, have courage and a heart. Pedler (1997) makes a valid argument that the practice of questioning and challenging can be difficult for organisations.

FURTHER READING

Pedler, M. (2012) *Action Learning for Managers.* Hampshire: Gower Publishing.

Pedler, M. and Abbott, C. (2013) *Facilitating Action Learning: A Practitioner's Guide.* Berkshire: Open University Press.

Revans, R. (2011) *ABC of Action Learning.* Farnham: Gower Publishing.

Part 3
Practice

Chapter 8
Being an action learner

PROFESSIONAL CAPABILITIES FRAMEWORK

This chapter will help you demonstrate the following capabilities:

- Critical Reflection and Analysis 6.3 – With support, rigorously question and evaluate the reliability and validity of information from different sources.
- Contexts and Organisations 8.5 – Understand and respect the role of others within the organisation and work effectively with them.
- Professional Leadership 9.2 – Recognise the value of, and contribute to, supporting the learning and development of others.

Introduction

This chapter introduces you to the process of action learning, how to prepare for a set meeting and what happens during the set meeting and in between. It introduces the role of the facilitator and how the facilitator supports the process. The skills of listening, questioning and giving feedback are explored. Finally we examine the skills learned by being in a set and that you can transfer into other areas of professional practice.

Action learning is an unusual innovation in education and learning because it is based on people doing their own research and tackling their own problems. In championing the learners and those actively engaged with practice, it is opposed to expert consultancy and traditional education practice. There has been a substantial growth in action learning activity over the last 20 years in the health sector and, in more recent years, the social care sector. In the health sector, action learning is well established and has been utilised in leadership development programmes, change and service improvement programmes. In the social care sector, action learning has begun to be mainstream, particularly encouraged by Skills for Care and The College of Social Work to support professional development in newly qualified social workers and to support the Professional Capabilities Framework. Although it could be argued that this use of action learning is a departure from Revans's original view of action learning tackling organisational issues, it does stay faithful to the cascade of learning back to the profession, thus developing both individuals and the profession of social work.

The purpose of action learning sets

The action learning set is at the heart of the action learning process and is the main vehicle for learning and action. It is in the action learning set that members consider and pursue their own actions in the workplace and consciously learn from the experience through a process of review, critical reflection and planning. The set provides the conditions where members learn from the challenges and problems they face in their work. Crucially, members of the set learn from reviewing past actions and their consequences, testing their own assumptions and planning the next steps. In learning together, they support and challenge each other to move into less familiar territories rather than sticking to past behaviours.

The action learning set process is designed to be a creative environment where you can share insights and learn from each other, create new relationships and strengthen existing ones, network and understand the positions of others, develop conditions for collaborative working and, lastly and crucially, provide space and time to consider the challenges of practice.

> *The set has become an integral part of my working life. The space gives me the energy boost I need to go back to work refreshed – being challenged about aspects of my practice is hard work but it gives me an inner resilience and resolve to see it through.*

(Social work manager)

What an action learning set looks like

The action learning set provides the time and space to attend to the relationship between reflection and action. Set members work together to help their colleagues to understand, explore and judge their situation and articulate future actions as a result. So, action learning sets are as individual as the members who take part. What an action learning set is not is a formal meeting, a seminar, a support group or a counselling or therapy group. There are some basic design criteria however:

- Action learning sets usually will have between four and seven people who agree to meet on a regular basis over a set period of time, e.g. once a month for six months. The length of the meeting will depend on the number of people present. A general rule of thumb for each person present is to allow 45 minutes, then add 30 minutes for beginnings and endings. So with five members the meeting will last about three to four hours and with six members a full day.

- Each set member will have a sponsor; this could be the manager or supervisor. The sponsor works with the participants to ensure that they are able to attend the sessions and is there to support and motivate them in the workplace. The key to success is that participants' development and the success of their work matters to both participant and sponsor.

- Both venue and dates of sessions will be scheduled in negotiation with the action learning set participants.

- There is likely to be a set facilitator or adviser, certainly in the early stages of the set.

The role of the facilitator or set adviser

In descriptions of action learning there is little mention of the set facilitator or set adviser. This is because the entire focus of the set is on its members' learning and action. The role is indeed controversial (Pedler and Abbott, 2013). It is easier to say what it is not; that is, the facilitator's role is not to teach, lead, act as expert consultant, manage or administer, chair the meeting or report to others what happens in the set.

David Casey (2011) attempted a description of the role of the facilitator that most practitioners would generally agree with:

> *Facilitate giving, facilitate receiving, clarify the various processes of action learning and help others take over tasks 1, 2 and 3.*

So you can expect your set facilitator or set adviser to help you and other set members ask questions, encourage you and other set members to listen, share information and exchange ideas, help the set to reflect collectively on the learning process that is happening in the set and help deal with any conflict that might impede the work of the set. There is more on the role of the facilitator and self-managed action learning sets in Chapter 9.

What happens in the set meeting?

There are three key activities in an action learning set:

1. Members support and challenge each other in order to develop a better understanding of a current challenge or problem. They do this through questioning their own and others' understanding of the situation and through that develop an insight to their situation.

2. Reflection on past action and the commitment to a new course of action.

3. Review and evaluation of how the set is operating together.

Set meeting content will vary depending on the group; however, it will follow a number of stages.

Stage 1: Catching up or checking in

This stage allows you and your fellow set members to share your immediate news from the workplace. It helps the group re-engage with each other and reform the group identity. It can also be useful to test the temperature, particularly within an organisation that is going through change.

Stage 2: Setting the agenda for the meeting

In most cases this will be a simple process of confirming the process and the order in which members present their issues. Sometimes because a set member has an issue that is urgent and complex, the set by agreement may change the rule of equal 'air time' in order to focus on one individual.

It is also the time when the ground rules are reaffirmed or modified.

Stage 3: Problem presentation or progress reporting

This is the stage where each member presents either progress on the problem/ challenge they presented at a previous meeting or a new problem/challenge. It is important to consider how you will present your challenge and completing a 'problem brief' will help you clarify your thoughts. You will be invited to present your problem/challenge and tell your colleagues what you would like from them. You will conclude your time slot with the actions you will take as a result of the discussion.

You have a range of options for how to present your problem/challenge and how the group might support and challenge you. We will outline some of these options in Chapter 9.

Stage 4: Review

At the end of the set meeting there will be a period of review and reflection. This review will cover the process and what you have learned as a group and as individuals. A set review sheet can help you to consolidate and reflect.

Table 8.1 Problem brief

Answer these questions to help you think through a problem, opportunity or issue for action learning:

1. Describe your problem situation in one sentence:
2. Why is this important?

   (i) to you?
   (ii) to your organisation/profession?

3. How will you recognise progress on this problem?
4. Who else would like to see progress on this problem?
5. What difficulties do you anticipate?
6. What are the benefits if this problem is reduced or resolved:

   (i) to you?

   (ii) to other people?

   (iii) to your organisation/profession?

Adapted from Pedler and Abbott (2013).

Table 8.2 Set review sheet

Each set member should spend five minutes reflecting on the work of the set before sharing their thoughts with fellow members on:

1. *My problem*

    The three key things I have learned about my problem today are:

2. *Myself*

    The one thing I've learned about myself today is:

3. *My profession*

    The one thing I have learned about being a social worker is:

4. *Action*

    My action steps before the next meeting are:

5. *Other set members*

    The most interesting thing I have learned today about the problems facing each of the other set members is:

Name:

Name:

Name:

Name:

6. *The set*

    The thing that stands out for me today in terms of the working of the set is:

Something we might do differently is:

Adapted from Pedler (2008).

An action learning problem

Revans was clear that the problem is the starting place for learning and action. Sometimes the word 'problem' is unhelpful: *in our organisation you are not allowed to have a problem – just a challenge* (social work manager). Problems can be seen to be too personal or even a weakness and for this reason we often use the word 'issue' or 'challenge'.

> *A problem in action learning is an issue, a concern, an opportunity or a task which you want to do something about.*

> (Pedler, 2011: 41)

Revans made the distinction between puzzle and problem. A puzzle may seem like a problem; however, there is somewhere a prescribed solution. Think about a crossword puzzle or a Sudoku puzzle: you may struggle to find the answer but there is one right answer and you will know that you have got it right when you find it.

Puzzles are characterised by an existing knowledge base of tried and tested solutions where there can be right answers and wrong answers. Puzzles can be addressed by programmed knowledge alone, although sometimes with the help of specialists or experts.

Knowing what form to complete following an incident on a home visit may be a problem for you but someone will know or there will be a procedure that you can refer to. So this would be termed a puzzle. How you manage the relationship with the family you have visited is a true action learning problem in that there will be no 'right' answer, but it is the starting point for enquiry and action.

So problems, in contrast to puzzles, are complex, rather than complicated; they are dynamic, not static, and often sit outside the organisation's hierarchies and systems.

> *Some problems are so complex that you have to be highly intelligent and well informed just to be undecided about them.*

> (attributed to Laurence J. Peter in Grint, 2005: 1468)

Grint (2005) uses the term 'wicked problem' to define those problems that require high levels of collaboration in areas of high uncertainty. 'Tame' problems are described as those that are amenable to planning, that is, have less requirement for collaboration and less uncertainty. Wicked problems are often those we have learned to live with or see as 'just too difficult'. For example, child or adult abuse, drug and alcohol problems in a particular town, poor communication between health and social care are all wicked problems that are highly complex and require collaboration between agencies and individuals.

Plsek and Greenhalgh (2004) have suggested that in health and social care there is a tendency to treat wicked problems as tame problems (puzzles):

> *Our learnt instinct . . . is to troubleshoot and fix things – in essence to break down the ambiguity, resolve any paradox, achieve more certainty and agreement and move into the simple system zone.*

In Chapter 2 we argued that social work is mainly concerned with messy, complex, dynamic situations and problems are unique to any one situation. Often in these cases, the problem is located in a number of different places and is seen differently by different people, so there is a need for high levels of collaboration. Programmed knowledge together with past experience of similar problems is the starting point in these situations; however formulas that worked in the past may not be appropriate or getting to the 'right answer' is not as important as getting collective consent to the next action. It is in these very cases that action learning can be applied.

Revans (1982: 715) described an action learning problem as meeting the following criteria.

- Is it real for you and others?

- Is it a genuine 'no-right-answer' situation?

- If you can create some movement on this issue, will you and others feel better?

In preparing for your set meeting, we offer you the template that will help you think about and prepare to present your problem (see Table 8.1 on page 112).

Ground rules

Action learning sets operate with a high level of trust and this community and the trust-building process start at the first set meeting with establishing the ground rules or the ways of working that the set agrees to adopt.

All members, including the facilitator, will take time to consider what is required to create a supportive learning environment. This can be seen as creating a learning contract with each other.

It is important to remember that the ground rules will be revisited at each meeting and there is an opportunity to discuss changes.

You are encouraged to take time, with each ground rule, to share what you understand it means and seek a common understanding with other members of the set. For example, confidentiality is often first on a set's list, but what does it mean? Can I talk about my action, thoughts and feelings to other people? Can I disclose the particular thing to my partner or supervisor?

Once the ground rules have been agreed members will need to decide how they will honour them. Often there is an assumption that this is the facilitator's role; however it is important that all members take ownership and responsibility for upholding, managing and reviewing their own ground rules.

Checklist: Potential ground rules

- Attendance
- Equality
- Responsibility for self
- Use 'I' language rather than 'we', 'you', e.g. 'We all know how difficult' becomes 'I know how difficult'
- Confidentiality
- Commitment
- Jargon
- All issues brought are relevant
- Being on time, prompt
- How to allocate time
- Breaks
- Note taking
- Honesty and openness
- Respect for self and others
- Duration of set and time of day
- How the set will work with the ground rules

Your role in supporting others

Sets vary greatly in their effectiveness and performance. You will be encouraged to urge others to aspire to action and learning that they would never achieve outside the set and the action learning process.

A highly successful set requires a good balance of support and challenge. These two qualities tend to be built up together within a set or group; ideally you would have high-quality support and high-quality challenge at the same time (Figure 8.1).

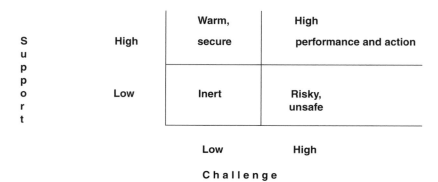

Figure 8.1 Support and challenge (Pedler and Abbott, 2013)

In a set where the support is very high but the challenge is low there is little commitment to action – this may be appropriate sometimes, especially when someone has taken a risky action that has resulted in unforeseen consequences! At the other extreme a set that offers high challenge to a colleague with little support can be threatening and it can feel unsafe to take risks, as the consequences of getting it wrong are too great.

There are various ways to build support and challenge, depending on the situation. Support can be more than just being listened to by others; challenge by a good question makes you think about what you are trying to do and why. These both seem deceptively simple and yet good listening and good questioning are often rare.

> *The set is the one safe place I can go and be really listened too. It feels a luxury in my work to have 45 minutes of undivided attention by a group of people who are actively listening and challenging me and I make much better decisions as a result of that.*

> (Social worker)

Good listening

The difficulty – and indeed rarity – of good listening was recognised by one of humanistic psychology's founders, Maslow:

> *To be able to listen, really wholly, passively, self effacingly listen without presupposing, classifying, improving, controverting, evaluating, approving or disapproving, without duelling with what is being said, without rehearsing the rebuttal in advance, without free associating to portions of what is being said so that the succeeding portions are not heard at all – such listening is rare.*

> (Maslow, 1969: 96)

The purpose of listening is to give your colleagues the time and space to describe their problem/challenge in their own way.

> *The power for me is having colleagues really paying me attention – my set really actively focuses on my problem, they don't think its stupid or easy – they pay what I say serious consideration and sometimes that's enough. I thought as a social worker I would be good at this but this process has made me realise that I am good at giving advice but not listening.*

> (Social worker)

It could be assumed that the social work profession would be expert at listening and asking questions but our experience is that social workers are often surprised how quickly they move from problem to suggested solutions. In an action learning set we assume that the person wants to resolve his or her own issues and jumping in with the solution can be unhelpful and even disrespectful.

LISTEN

When I ask you to listen to me and you start giving me advice, you have not done what I asked.

When I ask you to listen to me and you begin to tell me 'why' I shouldn't feel that way, you are trampling on my feelings.

When I ask you to listen to me and you feel you have to do something to solve my problems, you have failed me, strange as that may seem.

Listen! All I ask is that you listen; not talk, nor do – just hear me – I'm not helpless, maybe discouraged and faltering, but not helpless.

When you do something for me, that I can and need to do for myself, you contribute to my fear and weakness.

But when you accept as a simple fact that I do feel what I feel, no matter how irrational, then I quit trying to convince you and can get about the business of understanding.

What's behind this irrational feeling? When that's clear the answers are obvious and I don't need advice. Irrational feelings make sense when we understand what's behind them.

Perhaps that's why prayer works sometimes for some people; because God is mute, and doesn't give advice to try to 'fix' things, He/She just listens, and lets you work it out for yourself.

So please listen, and just hear me, and if you want to talk, wait a minute for your turn,

And I'll listen to you.

This poem was written by a mental health consumer who was institutionalised over a number of years in Queensland, Australia. He wishes to remain anonymous.

Active listening can be a difficult skill to practise – here are some things you can try.

Paraphrase

Let your colleagues know that you have heard them by using some of their words or metaphors when you feed back to them or ask a question, e.g. 'I think I heard you say that . . .'.

Clarify understanding

It is easy to assume you understand what your colleague means – checking shows that you are listening and care about your co-worker's frame of reference. 'I hate it when . . .' could be responded with: 'Hate is a strong word, what do you mean by that?'

Physical position

Try to keep an open position – arms unfolded, looking towards the person talking, and maintaining appropriate eye contact. If you want to make notes, ask permission.

Attitude

Try to stop your own thoughts or self-talk. One way to do this is to repeat the words you are hearing to yourself; this can stop your own thoughts wandering. Be aware that the feelings you are having in relation to your colleague's problem/challenge are your own, and not theirs. Be aware of your colleague's body language and tone of voice as well as what he or she is saying.

Finally

Remember that silence is very powerful. Try leaving pauses in the conversation. As we have seen in Chapter 1, much has been written about how action learning ideas have a foundation in Quakerism. In Quakerism, the purpose of silence is seen as identifying striving for truth in the individual and then finding a way of reconciling this truth with action in the world. By leaving silence, the set member has time to think and reflect and often comes forward with important ideas.

Good questions

Nobel Prize winner Isidor Isaac Rabi credited his success to learning how to ask good questions. 'Every other Jewish mother in Brooklyn would ask her child after school, "So, did you learn anything today?" But not my mother 'Izzy'. She would say, "Did you ask a good question today?"' (Rabi, 1993).

Good questions come from our ability to listen effectively. Good questions help set members to deepen their understanding or their view of their problem or challenge and take responsibility for them to work on it themselves rather than be given solutions.

Argyris and Schön (1996) identified two types of questions – what they call Model 1 and Model 2.

Model 1 questions are designed in such a way as to:

- get the other person to agree with one's own view;
- advocate one's own view in a manner that limits others' questioning of it;
- evaluate the other person's view and attribute causes to it.

Model 2 questions are designed to:

- actively enquire into the other person's views and the reasoning supporting them;
- advocate one's views and reasoning in a way that encourages others to confront them and to help the speaker discover where the view may be mistaken;
- state publicly the inferences that one makes about others and the data that leads to those inferences, and invite others to correct the inferences if they are inaccurate.

Arguably we tend to use Model 1 questions in our day-to-day interactions with others but action learning creates an opportunity to use Model 2 questions. In an action learning set you ask questions in response to a fellow set member's presentation of a problem or challenge in practice. Your aim is to find those questions that help your colleagues gain new insight – help them question themselves, especially on aspects they may not have considered previously. In addition to developing your own insight through this process, the set also gains an insight into how it operates and is developing.

Revans (Pedler, 2008: 73) noted three questions as being good to start with:

1. *Who knows* . . . about the problem?
2. *Who cares* . . . about the problem?
3. *Who can* . . . do anything about the problem?

They refer to three central processes in human action – thinking, feeling and willing. Professional education often focuses on the thinking – Do I understand the problem? or Have I analysed it properly? It is here that we can often get stuck and suffer 'paralysis by analysis', unable to move to action. Action learners understand that how you feel about the problem and how committed you are to action are just as important, or even maybe more so.

Thinking questions

This is traditionally thought of as associated with the head, and is termed *cognitive* by psychologists. The focus is on what happens 'in the head'. The purpose of the questioning, listening and reflecting is to get a more detailed picture of the situation and people involved by exploring data, facts, stories, information, assumptions and alternatives:

- What have you done so far?
- When was the last time this happened?
- What is the service user/family saying to you?
- How much time are you spending on this problem?
- What makes this problem so challenging?
- What made that meeting so difficult?
- Who else is involved?
- Who has the final decision on the outcome?
- How important is it to them that this problem is resolved?
- Whose help do you need?
- What does your practice supervisor say to you?
- If this was a case study as part of your degree, how would you answer it?
- Who has specialist knowledge?
- Can you see a pattern emerging?
- What sense are you making from the feedback you are receiving?
- Is there a pattern in the way the case is being managed?

Feeling questions

These are traditionally associated with the heart, termed *affective* by psychologists. The focus is on the emotions and power behind the words. The purpose of the questioning, listening and reflecting is to support, empathise, nurture, challenge and confront the problem holder.

- Why is this problem/challenge so important to you?
- How did you feel when you heard that?
- How did you feel when your professional judgement was challenged by the family?
- What is the person doing that makes you react in this way?
- Would you be surprised if the service user felt the same/differently?
- How do you feel about the questions you have been asked in this group?
- What other reasons could there be to explain why he/she did that?
- You say that your supervisor would not be interested – what makes you say that?
- What is stopping you . . .?
- You said last time that you were going to raise the issue with your manager, and you haven't! What can you do to make sure this happens next time?

Willing questions

These are traditionally thought of as limbs, particularly hands, and are termed *conative* by psychologists. They focus on the drive, motivation and determination to get things done. The purpose of the questioning, listening and reflecting is to look ahead and take action by finding direction, planning and setting goals or alternatively, taking stock, reviewing, reflecting and evaluating.

- Can you describe how things will be in one year, five years, ten years?
- How will you decide what action to take?
- What help or support might you need?
- How will you get that support?
- What alternatives are there?
- What will you do next?
- If you plan is accepted, how will you tell the team?
- What shall we do at the next meeting?
- Could we structure it differently?
- How could we do things differently?
- What have you achieved since the last meeting?
- What made this happen?
- What are the things you have learned from the experience?
- What have we achieved as a group?
- What has helped?
- What could we do more of/less of?
- How could you create similar opportunities back at work?
- What conditions have helped us/you learn?

The aim of the questions is always to support your colleagues in the set to question themselves, which is the process that fosters insight. The question is selfless, not asked to highlight how clever, more senior or more powerful you are, but as a way for set members to explore their own view of the problem or challenge.

The adviser or facilitator will model asking questions and use various approaches to help you gain this skill and avoid unhelpful questions.

Unhelpful questions can include the following.

Leading questions

These questions put the answer or advice in the question, e.g. 'Do you think that it would be a good idea to talk to the parents with a counsellor present?'

Multiple questions

These questions are several questions rolled into one and the temptation is that the person being questioned answers the first or the easiest, e.g. 'When did you meet your practice supervisor, what did she say when you told her and how did you feel about that?'

Closed questions

These are questions that can be answered 'yes' or 'no' and restrict the set member's options for response. However, they do have uses, for example in checking factual information: 'Can I just clarify that Joe is your manager?'

Long-drawn-out questions

If the question is too long and overly complex then the set member can lose the meaning.

Overly probing questions

Although asking challenging questions is encouraged when the set is relatively new, overly challenging questions that the set member is not ready to address can be threatening.

Trick questions

These are questions that can trip set members up or expose them unnecessarily, e.g. 'Can we assume that you have not read the new policy on client confidentiality which addresses this question?'

The more skilled you are with the various action learning processes, the more likely it is that you will want to have a go at self-facilitating your set, with members taking on the role in turn or carrying it out collectively.

PRACTICE EXAMPLE

When we first met as a set we had a facilitator. She used different methods to help us explore problems and by example showed us the sort of questions that were helpful, and those that were not! After four meetings, she suggested that we didn't need her and we self-facilitate – we didn't think we could so instead she brought a problem to the group and asked us to facilitate. We realised then just how much we had learned about the process and after that we carried on as a self-facilitated group.

(Social work manager)

Checklist: Being an effective set member

- Prepare for the meeting.
- Be clear in your own mind about what you want to achieve from your time. What do you need from the set today?
- Think about how much you need to say to explain how things are going.
- Explain this as clearly as you can. (Sometimes you may want to ask the set to help you think through something you feel confused about.)
- Try to stay within your time limit.
- Point out to the set what is not helpful to you.

Develop action points and . . .

- Work on them before the next meeting.
- Reflect on your learning and share it with others.

When supporting:

- Keep the focus on the person who is presenting and on his or her learning.
- Listen actively.
- Stick to the ground rules and challenge others if they do not.
- Be supportive – show interest and empathy.
- Learn not to interrupt.
- Ask helpful questions.
- Ask for clarification.
- Be honest, open and specific in your feedback while being sensitive.
- Treat diversity and equality issues seriously.
- Provide information if requested.
- Offer insights and ideas tentatively and at the right time.
- Take responsibility for your own learning.
- Collaborate with others in their learning.
- Speak for yourself.
- Avoid sweeping generalisations.
- Accept that someone else's solution may be different from your own.

(Adapted from Beaty *et al.*, 1993)

Feedback

During the process of all individuals presenting their challenge or problem there will be an opportunity for you to give feedback to your colleague. This does not mean just positive feedback; negative feedback given skilfully can be just as important.

Feedback will be of little value to the presenter unless it is given in a way that the presenter can accept, understand and use. The prospect of receiving feedback can often create fear in the receiver and the ability to receive the information may be switched off as a defence mechanism. So in giving feedback it is important to take into account the receiver's emotional state. It is useful to check that the feedback has been received and if appropriate may be recorded in some way.

Research by London (1997) suggests that helpful and effective feedback enables the receiver to self-assess more accurately and seek feedback again. It is possible to develop feedback skills by practising both clarity and simplicity of the message. Positive feedback is often rare, partly because we may take for granted a person's skills or qualities or alternatively we are embarrassed to say something positive in case it does not seem authentic or for fear it may be misinterpreted. Watch the news on the television or read the papers and as a profession social workers are often in receipt of negative feedback; many social workers report that supervision also can focus on what hasn't gone well in a case. In our experience the process of learning from success (see Chapter 9) can be very powerful and motivating. Set members often find it hard to give negative feedback as they feel they are the 'bearer of bad news'; however, negative feedback stored up which then explodes under pressure is destructive and leads to no change in the presenter's practice.

Guidelines in giving effective feedback

Clarity

Be clear about what you want to say. First, observe and listen carefully to the presenter. Then record your observations in concrete and specific terms about what you saw and heard.

Own the feedback

Start the feedback with 'I' or 'In my view' rather than 'You are', which suggests a universal opinion. By owning the feedback you are taking responsibility for what you are saying.

Start with the positive

We all need encouragement and it is important to know what was effective, so do not take the positives for granted. So start with, for example, 'I liked the way you looked up the latest research on Lewy body dementia before you visited Mrs X; it informed your approach.'

Be specific

General comments are not usually helpful in feedback – phrases like 'You were brilliant' or 'That was awful' may be nice or not to hear but they do not give the data to change behaviour. For example, 'What I liked about the way you approached your supervisor was that you were very clear about what was needed to resolve the case.'

Focus on behaviour rather than the person

Your feedback cannot change the person, for example, the individual's attributes or accent, but you can influence the behaviour by giving effective feedback. For example, 'I noted that you did not respond to the question about approaching the care home manager and I wondered why.'

Review

At the end of the set meeting there will be a period of review, both individual and collective. Useful questions to consider are:

- Were real problems being addressed here today?
- Were ideas being tested in action?
- What evidence is there of learning:
  - as personal development?
  - in the set as a collective?
  - organisational or professional?

Table 8.2 on page 113 provides a format you might find helpful in your review individually and collectively, especially in the early stages of the set.

Skills that are developed in action learning

Many valuable skills are developed through practising action learning. In this chapter, we have seen that there are the roles of presenting an issue or challenge, challenging and supporting others with their issues or challenges and facilitating the process.

Pedler (2008) identified the skills that you can develop in each of these areas as:

1. *Presenting* a problem:

- Taking and holding the focus of the set;
- Analysing and describing a problem;
- Asking for help, advice, assistance;
- Being able to receive – help, advice, feedback, challenge;
- Ability to reflect on what you receive and experience;

- Staying in charge of your time, problem, learning;
- Planning next steps;
- Proactivity (a tendency to initiate action);
- Skills in organisational politics;
- Resilience and perseverance;
- Self-belief.

2. *Helping* others with their problems:

- Belief in others (in their ability to understand the world in their way, take action on their problem);
- Empathy;
- Credulous listening (ability to listen to others and suspend your own evaluations);
- Ability to give – help, advice, assistance;
- Questioning;
- Supporting;
- Challenging;
- Generating options for action;
- Willingness to support outside the set.

3. *Facilitating* the process

- Facilitating members' giving to and receiving from each other;
- Ability to summarise and draw the 'big picture';
- Understanding of learning processes in individuals, groups and organisations;
- Understanding of the micropolitics of the organisation;
- Ability to question self and admit uncertainties and errors.

All of these skills might broadly be defined as learning skills (though some are more tendencies, abilities or qualities). Their purpose is to help people move round the action and learning cycle.

Chapter summary

- The purpose of action learning in social work is to support taking action and learning from messy, complex 'wicked problems'.
- Action learning sets and how they work will vary but follow a similar structure.

- The facilitator role is useful at the start of the set, but not essential.

- Preparation for the set meeting and presenting a challenge or issue is important.

- The role of support and challenge through listening and questioning in the set is crucial to insightful learning.

- Action learning can support the development of the skills of presenting challenges or issues, supporting and challenging others and facilitating.

FURTHER READING

Pedler, M. (2008) *Action Learning for Managers.* Gower Press.

Chapter 9
Facilitating action learning

PROFESSIONAL CAPABILITIES FRAMEWORK

This chapter will help you demonstrate the following capabilities:

- Professionalism 1.9 – Demonstrate a commitment to your continuous learning and development.
- Professionalism 1.10 – With support, take steps to manage and promote own safety, health, wellbeing and emotional resilience.
- Professional Leadership 9.1 – Recognise the importance of, and begin to demonstrate, professional leadership as a social worker.
- Professional Leadership 9.2 – Recognise the value of, and contribute to, supporting the learning and development of others.

Introduction

Facilitation in action learning can be helpful for those sets that need an injection of enthusiasm, support in modelling appropriate questions to set members and also to keep the set on track. The chapter will establish three key roles of the facilitator: the 'accoucheur' or initiator, the 'combiner' and the facilitator of organisational learning. These roles, described by Pedler and Abbott (2013), highlight that set facilitation is not always preferred. However, it is argued that facilitation can support action learning sets provided that the facilitator becomes acutely aware of his or her power and influence and learns not to become a teacher.

The literal definition of facilitation is to 'make easy, ease, smooth the progress' and few experienced set facilitators would agree that action learning set facilitation is that. Definitions of action learning do not mention the word facilitator but focus on the action learning set, the members, the challenges they bring to the set and the learning they take from taking action on the problem. The facilitator role had no place in Revans's early writings and when it did in the 1970s Revans was keen to express his doubts by limiting the role to being a combiner – to create the conditions to get action learning started, describing them as 'supernumeraries'. Revans was always dubious about the need for a facilitator because he feared that people calling themselves facilitators would develop an identity of their own and therefore start to call themselves experts in their own right. Revans predicted that educators may start to call themselves facilitators and, whilst he welcomed the idea, he doubted that they would change and they would continue to use their 'expert status'. Because of this, he was at pains to stress that action learning set members, individually and collectively, should control their own affairs, so as to avoid *yet another round of dependence upon ambiguous facilitators* (Revans, 2011: 9). This view of facilitators together with current thinking lends an ambiguity to the role and can lead to some anxiety for facilitators as to know whether they are *doing it right* (Pedler and Abbott, 2008).

Revans's position is controversial, and despite his misgivings, most action learning sets will have facilitators at least to begin with. In our experience, there are those that successfully move from facilitated to self-facilitated, but it is far less common to start as self-facilitated sets, even amongst sets of facilitators!

Various reasons are cited for this:

- a lack of understanding among set members about the process of action learning;

- a need for help for set members to get to know each other;

- a need for someone who is responsible for helping the group in their action and learning;

- the lack of skills for set members to facilitate themselves;

- the expectations of participants or sponsors.

The three roles of the facilitator

Pedler and Abbott (2013) identified three roles for the facilitator, shown in Figure 9.1.

The first, that of initiator of action learning, is closest to Revans's view of the facilitator role. This is also the role that is less visible to the participants of an

Figure 9.1 The three roles of the action learning adviser (adapted from Pedler and Abbott (2013))

action learning set, in that it is concerned with the culture of learning in an organisation, testing its readiness, the influencing and persuading of the organisation or team to embrace the concepts, the design of the intervention, seeking sponsors and participants.

The second role is that of facilitating sets and is the subject of this chapter.

The third is the role of organisational or professional learning and how this is fed back into the organisation or profession.

The facilitation role educator

In Revans's formula $L = P + Q$ practice education and supervision are, as we have seen in Chapter 1, largely based on Revans's P – traditional knowledge or instruction. One of the problems that many new to action learning facilitation face is that they come from a background of teachers or trainers and their skill set is based on the skills that are designed to facilitate P.

As we have seen, action learning, although not dismissing P as unimportant, focuses on Q or questioning insight. Some of the problems in sets arise because the facilitator is unable to drop the learned skills of teaching and acquire the new skills of facilitation.

> *I had been in an action learning set before but this was different. The facilitator dominated and used every problem a person brought to give a mini lecture on personalisation. I think they thought they were being helpful and it generated discussion around the subject but avoided the person's real problem with the implementation and how they could move forward. I went away feeling really disappointed at losing the opportunity to learn from real problems.*

(Action learning set member)

> *I was learning to facilitate action learning sets and went to support an experienced facilitator run a large-scale event that would result in a number of action learning sets being formed. I found it almost impossible to walk in the room without a lesson plan, Powerpoint slides, a pile of papers. Here was this person with a process and some props – a flip chart, some index cards and saying 'we work with what is important to them [the participants]'. I was completely insecure and felt out of my depth.*

(New facilitator)

Take a moment to consider the two accounts above in terms of your own practice as a practice supervisor or practice educator. Where are you currently on the spectrum of educator to facilitator? Then try the questionnaire in Activity 9.1.

ACTIVITY 9.1

In this tool, there are two lists of skills: those needed for teaching P, and those needed to facilitate Q. Check out these two lists in terms of your own skills set.

Step 1

Look down this list and put a tick or a cross in the box depending upon whether:

✓ *you have this skill or special knowledge*

✗ *you do not have this skill or special knowledge.*

List A

- *Expert knowledge of subject matter related to action learning problems* ☐
- *Are able to avoid topics outside your areas of expertise* ☐
- *Familiarity and full understanding of the task environment in which set members are operating* ☐
- *The ability to teach practical methods and procedures for problem solving* ☐
- *The ability to question in a way that leads to set members arriving at the 'right' answer* ☐
- *Presentational and teaching skills – good delivery, and clear sequencing of inputs; reinforcing correct responses* ☐
- *Maintaining the pace – managing resistance to ideas and moving on* ☐
- *Being helpful – helping people resolve their problems* ☐

Step 2

Look down this second list, and repeat the same procedure as before in Step 1, putting a tick or a cross in the box depending upon whether:

✓ *you have this skill or special knowledge*

✗ *you do not have this skill or special knowledge.*

List B

- *Encourage set members to learn from the experience of each other* ☐
- *Design opportunities for members to find their own answers* ☐
- *Encourage a climate which is both supportive and challenging* ☐

- *Can refrain from displaying your own knowledge and understanding* ☐

- *Challenge the assumptions members have about their tasks and organisations* ☐

- *Help members give difficult feedback to each other* ☐

- *Ask questions that will help members explore their issues and the assumptions behind their actions* ☐

- *Raise difficult issues and conflicts, even if this results in discomfort for you and others* ☐

- *Acknowledge mistakes in facilitation openly, framing them as learning opportunities* ☐

- *Encourage members to take on the tasks of facilitating the set* ☐

Step 3

Consider the results in light of the examples given above and make some notes on your position on the spectrum between teaching and facilitation. Has it confirmed anything? Changed anything?

Discuss both sets of questionnaire results with your colleagues. Go down each list considering each item in turn:

- *Is there evidence of this in your behaviour within the set?* ☐

- *Should you try to do this less or more?* ☐

Step 4

Make some notes for an action plan for your future work as a facilitator in the action learning set.

Good facilitators come in all shapes and sizes. However most will have in common a bias towards certain sorts of behaviour, for example, asking questions; and a bias against certain others, for example, extended teaching in the set. There are numerous lists of facilitation skills, including attending, listening, empathising, reflecting, questioning, responding, intervening, giving feedback and summarising. These facilitation skills apply equally in action learning but with an additional twist; the facilitator personally needs all these abilities, but is also responsible for helping the set members to acquire them for themselves.

Casey (1976) echoed this notion by describing the role of the facilitator as:

1. facilitating giving;

2. facilitating receiving;

3. clarifying the various processes of action learning;

4. helping others take over tasks 1, 2 and 3.

O'Hara *et al.* (2004: 36) suggest a range of skills for members:

- questioning skills – to help people to find their own solutions to their problems;

- active listening skills – to communicate to people that they were being understood, to help them work out their own solutions but not give solutions, to help them clarify their situation, the facts, their thoughts, and their feelings and to hear without judging or evaluating;

- the ability to give and receive feedback – to help people learn and develop, to increase their self-esteem and to make them feel valued;

- an understanding of group process – to appreciate the difference between task and process and between helpful and sabotaging behaviours;

- creative problem-solving skills – to provide a range of tools to help the set when they were 'stuck';

- the skill of reflection – to plan for future action and to help derive the learning from action; and

- understanding the process of learning – to enable people to appreciate the variety of ways in which people can learn.

By focusing on set membership skills we change the discussion about facilitation. Following Revans (1998: 12), the purpose of this development of skills in set members is to enable them to become self-facilitating or, as often happens, the facilitator becomes a set member in his or her own right.

REFLECTION POINT

If you apply Casey's notion in your facilitation practice, at what point would you become a set member and bring your own issue to the set?

This question was asked of facilitators taking part in a development programme for social workers supporting newly qualified social workers (NQSWs).

The answers were revealing. Sixty per cent felt that this would be something they would not do, for reasons including complexity of caseload; their issues were management ones and therefore not appropriate; they were more senior and it would make them feel vulnerable; and they felt they should know the answers. Those who said they would gave their reasons as because they felt the fresh eyes of an NQSW would give them new insight, would refresh their own knowledge, and would demonstrate the values of social work. They also commented that it was important that newly qualified staff recognised that, no matter how experienced you were, there were still problems that you either hadn't met before or were complex and needed a new way of thinking. In doing this it would encourage staff to share issues rather than believe they could handle everything themselves. This demonstration of social and emotional intelligence, as we have seen in Chapter 4, allows practitioners to be more open with issues they are anxious about and that are therefore a barrier to their learning.

There are no rules for being a good facilitator; however, there are basic guidelines.

Skilled facilitators

- Ask more questions:
    - What are you trying to do?
    - What is stopping you?
    - Who, or what, can help?
- Encourage giving and receiving of members in the set by encouraging listening, questioning, sharing and exchanging ideas with each other.
- Bring to the surface conflicts in the group, by making it acceptable to talk about blocks or barriers to action.
- Make learning processes explicit – by encouraging people to 'learn how to learn'.
- Encourage action, and a belief and confidence that individually and collectively the group as a whole will succeed in their goals.

ACTIVITY 9.2

The skilled action learning facilitator is able to:

- *gain the trust of all members;*
- *create a safe environment in which people can begin to take risks;*

- *point out learning opportunities;*

- *encourage openness and sharing;*

- *ensure that everyone is listened to;*

- *help people learn how to ask good questions;*

- *model constructive challenge;*

- *encourage members to experiment both within the set, and outside, with clients, other agencies and colleagues;*

- *propose reviews and evaluations from time to time;*

- *reward appropriate reflections, results and changes;*

- *promote awareness of the learning process in the set;*

- *know when to leave the set to be self-facilitating;*

- *foster the image of a high-performing group.*

Using the list above as a checklist:

- *Which of these do you think you are achieving with the set you are working with?*

- *Which of these do you think you are not achieving with the set you are working with?*

- *What action is suggested as a result of this analysis?*

Self-facilitated groups

As we have seen, set facilitators are encouraged to review their place in the set and at some point remove themselves so that the set can become self-facilitating. There are two ways of doing this. Either one person volunteers to facilitate a full set meeting or members take it in turns during the set meeting:

> *Each set member takes and shares responsibility for facilitation as part of their set membership. Only when they are being presenter will they relinquish that responsibility.*

(McGill and Beaty, 2001)

In either case it is useful to build into the meeting time for reviewing the facilitation.

You may like to try the following in your set meeting as a way of encouraging members to start managing their own facilitation.

Step 1
Ask for one set member to volunteer to be the facilitator, whilst another is talking about his or her project.

Step 2
Whilst working with the presenter of the problem, set members also make some notes about the facilitation process.

Step 3
At the end of that particular presenter's time, the set briefly feeds back to the facilitator what they appreciated and what they thought was helpful, and what they thought was less helpful or could be improved.

Step 4
After hearing from all set members, the volunteer set adviser makes some notes for future reference and relinquishes the role.

This process could be repeated until all members have had a turn or could take place every meeting with one or two volunteers until the group feels comfortable to manage their own meetings.

There are various alternatives to this process; the most obvious is that members can take it in turn to facilitate the whole of one meeting at which they would not take any time for themselves.

Whichever method is chosen, working through this process will help all set members develop the skills and awareness of the set adviser, and it will enable the set as a whole greatly to expand its capacity to facilitate itself.

Pre-set preparation

There are a number of logistical matters to manage before the set meets, including:

- arranging and checking the venue;
- access for the less able;
- transport and/or parking facilities;
- arranging refreshments;
- checking the times of the meeting;
- contacting set members with the arrangements.

This may be carried out by an administrator if you are facilitating an in-house set or in a multi-disciplinary set the responsibilities may be shared across hosting organisations. You may consider rotating venues in these circumstances. This gives each set member a sense of each other's working environments. In these circumstances set members often take on the responsibility for the hosting arrangement as they know their organisation. It can be a useful way towards self-management of the set. You may also want to send out a pre-meeting preparation brief to set members to help them focus on a problem to bring to the set meeting: see Table 8.1 on page 112 for an example.

Creating a learning space

Edmonstone (2003) notes that the consequences of a poor environment or of not protecting the boundaries of the set can destroy the quality of space needed.

> *We ended up using one member's office, which seemed like a good idea at the time . . . [but] it may have been a false economy. We were at work after all . . . [and] I couldn't switch into learning mode easily. The person whose office it was, was good about switching phones off, etc., but it didn't stop people wandering in with 'As you are here, could you look at this?'. At breaks it was noticeable that we all rushed off to 'just photocopy', 'just make a telephone call', 'just sort xyz out'.*

> *We first met in a community centre – It was very pleasant, the staff very friendly, the food superb. The location was good for everyone. The only problem was that the room was used as a crèche/playgroup three days a week, so was full of toys, etc. I never felt comfortable – it reminded me of home, I wanted to start tidying up!*

> *The drive to the party was good – as I drove down the main avenue I was getting nearer to my learning and further away from the workplace. Knowing I couldn't be contacted [no signal] made it even more so. Each tree passing meant less contact/interference.*

(Pedler and Abbott, 2008)

The importance of the space chosen for the action learning set is illustrated above both in terms of an environment free from distraction as well as the value of surroundings being a 'communicative space' where people can make sense of the tensions and the demands of their situations and their own views on life as they would like to live it (Mead, 2006: 159, 161). Mead argues that, without this quality of space, people are less able to undertake the emotional labour of making sense of their situations and the tensions therein.

Set meeting process

There is no fixed pattern to a set meeting and individual sets will create their own ways of working. However, they often include:

- *Catch-up* – this is a good way of starting because it helps to pull the set back together. There are various ways of doing this but time keeping can be an issue. Usually it is a short round where members can share with each other the actions and developments since the previous meeting.

- *Setting the meeting agenda* – including establishing a 'running order' of turn taking; and while many sets have the ground rule of equal time for members, this may be modified by agreement here depending on the urgency and/or complexity of individual issues.

- *Presenting* – each member takes a turn to present challenges or problems and receive questions and feedback. This takes up most of the meeting time and usually starts with progress from the last meeting and describing the issue as they see it now, being offered questions and getting feedback from other set members, considering their options and committing to actions they will take before the next meeting.

- *Learning review* – where members review their learning, individually and collectively as a set.

Ground rules

Ground rules are an action and learning contract agreed between the set members. They are ways of working together which enable the set to do their work well and that reflect action learning values. Ground rules should be considered as provisional and open to change. They can be revisited at any meeting to consider whether they are still relevant.

Each set creates its own ground rules to shape the way they will work over the cycle of meetings. What do we need as rules to create a supportive but challenging learning environment?

Table 9.1 lists some examples from Pedler and Abbott (2013).

Confidentiality and respect for each other often come at the top of lists, and can usefully be tested by the facilitator: what, exactly do we mean by respect for each other? What do we mean by confidentiality, between whom?

Table 9.1 Some ground rules

Practical	Behavioural
• Attendance and punctuality	• Confidentiality
• The duration of meetings and breaks	• Commitment
• Declaration of conflicts of interest	• Respect for and between each other
• Reviewing the ground rules	• Non-judgemental
• Note taking – who owns the notes and what happens to any notes taken	• Being responsible for self
• Each person to have equal voice and time	• Using 'I' not 'we' – so 'we all know that' becomes 'I know that'
• How the set celebrates achievement or their time together	• Support and challenging each other
• The use of jargon	• The right to say 'no' or to decline to respond to a question or challenge

Asking these questions may highlight that what seems simple is not. In one case, a set member's behaviour in a previous set meeting was discussed in the set. A fellow set member had felt that the first set member had challenged her inappropriately and had discussed this with him outside the set meeting. The first set member was absent from the group during this discussion and when it was reported back, felt the ground rules of both respect and confidentiality had been broken and his trust in the group and the facilitator had broken down. There is perhaps always a danger present for such occurrences, but by testing assumptions and the limits of what is taken for granted, the facilitator can help the set to develop a shared understanding of the meaning of each rule.

Questioning

Questioning insight comes when new insight is gained through members being helped to question themselves and their situations, especially on issues that they may not have previously considered. Revans's three questions (1982: 715) can be asked in relation to any situation:

1. Who knows about (understands) this problem?

2. Who cares about it?

3. Who can do anything about it?

These connect with three central processes of human action: thinking, feeling and willing (see Chapter 8).

Balancing support and challenge

In Chapter 8 the concept of balancing support and challenge in the set is discussed. One of the problems that can occur in a set is that, after it has matured, it can settle down rather too much, and end up in a rut. Or there is a temptation to attempt too much challenge too early. Revans said that warmth comes before light, and to up the level of challenge in a set requires a higher level of support.

As a facilitator it is important to test the temperature of the set periodically. One way to do this is to ask the group on the two dimensions of Figure 9.2 and then ask them what they think about the consequences of the group climate and how it relates to their work.

Step 1

Draw the chart below on a sheet of flipchart paper. Just draw the main dimensions and label them; leave out the box titles.

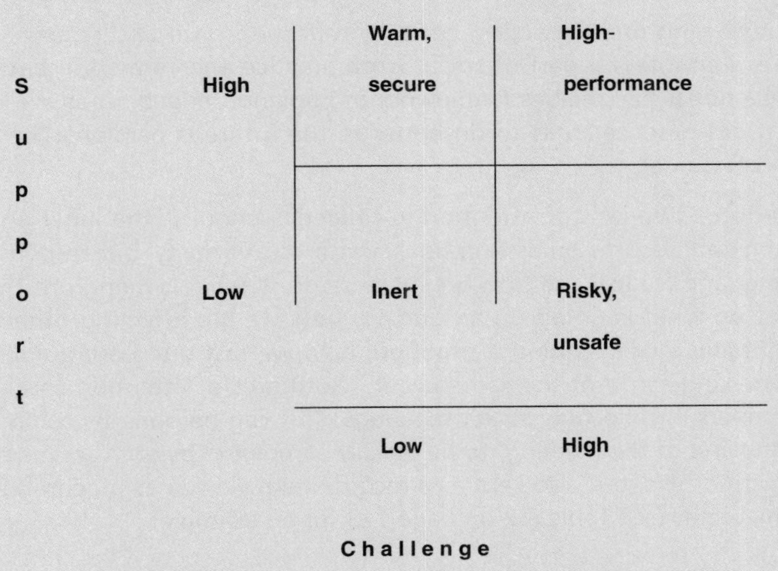

```
                        Warm,         High-
    S           High    secure        performance

    u

    p

    p

    o           Low     Inert         Risky,

    r                                 unsafe

    t

                        Low           High
```

Challenge

Figure 9.2 Temperature check exercise

Step 2

Ask each person in turn to put a cross on the chart to indicate the position they think the set has been operating in for the last hour, or meeting, or even the last few meetings.

Step 3

When everyone has put their cross on the paper, discuss the data you have produced. Does it indicate that the set is too risky? Too comfortable? Or what?

As an alternative approach, you can ask people to draw their own grid and make their own private mark, and then:

- *go to the public stage of putting all their crosses on one sheet; or*

- *have a short discussion in pairs, without making individual assessments public; before*

- *moving to a general discussion.*

Step 4

What action does the set need to take in the light of the discussion?

Reflecting, reviewing, recording

In social work, reviewing one's practice, critically reflecting on it and recording learning points is a an integral part of social work practice and forms the backbone of the Professional Capabilities Framework in England. Indeed, in all walks of life, learning from practice so as to do better in the future is part of what it means to be a professional.

Marshall (2001) notes two arcs of attention in reflective enquiry, the inner and the outer. The inner arc focuses on assumptions, patterns of activity, our response to others, the language we use and how we make sense of what is going on. The outer arc focuses on what is going on around us, how we are affecting others, how we are maintaining or changing a situation, how we test our assumptions, how others are making sense of the same event. Both arcs of attention can be useful to set members in reflecting on set meetings. This can be done by using a review sheet at the end of the meeting, to be quickly completed by each set member and shared with others, but also kept as a record and reviewed as preparation for subsequent meetings (see Table 8.2 on page 113 for an example).

Some processes to use

During an action learning set it is important to ensure that the conversations are structured and that a strict allocation of time is adhered to. This will avoid the set transforming into a discussion group, or digression, and will keep the set members engaged. Although action learning sets should be led by the participants, sometimes it is helpful to try out a process that might be helpful. The following are all processes that have been used successfully with social workers and we have included some examples from our own practice.

Learning from success

Participants in action learning sets are primarily concerned with problems and things they want to change. Sometimes it is worth breaking out of this pattern by considering a success story and investigating what was learned for the success. It is often difficult for participants to contribute a true success story and tell it with pride. This is often true when the profession is highlighted in the media when things go wrong and where the supervision received focuses on problem-solving cases going badly. However, it can be very instructive and enjoyable to reflect together regularly on things which – sometimes surprisingly – went well.

PRACTICE EXAMPLE

I took a problem to an action learning set about a case that involved engaging with two agencies to offer services to one of my clients. It wasn't complex and I couldn't understand why I wasn't getting the

---

results I expected. My supervisor was putting pressure on me to close the case. The facilitator suggested I talk about a similar case that had gone really well – at first I couldn't see how that would help. The set were asked to focus on what I had done and what the context had been when they asked questions. It was embarrassing to talk about a success story as it really is our daily work and I am just not used to talking about these things. The set then made a list of all the success factors and it became apparent that the difference was obvious between this and the case I was dealing with. One of the agencies was new to the social services team and the reason I had been successful before was the strong relationship with the agencies involved. So, my action was to spend time with this agency and build a relationship with them rather than assuming, as I had done previously, that they understood our processes. It was simple but it worked.

(NQSW 2011)

Five steps

This method supports the testing of assumptions that the problem holder may have about a case. It also helps the set participants understand the relevance of questions. Following the presentation of a problem, a round of questions is asked by set members and then each member of the set proposes a definition of the problem. The problem holder then revisits the nature of the problem and restates it before the session begins again.

PRACTICE EXAMPLE

My role is to coordinate the support and training of newly qualified staff and my problem was getting managers to be motivated – they just didn't seem to be interested no matter what I did. There were lots of excuses, mainly time and workload. I am enthusiastic by this work – how can I get them to be? One of the definitions offered really struck me: 'There is no common understanding of the accountability and responsibilities between you and the managers for supporting NQSWs.' I was prepared for lots of suggestions to what I could do but it occurred to me that unless I clarified the assumptions about accountability and responsibility none would work. The problem I bought to the group was a symptom of a bigger problem that needed addressing – so that's what I did.

(Assessed and supported year in employment manager)

Sitting in the corner or gossip

Following the presentation of the issue, the problem holder moves away from the group to listen to other participants explore the range of issues, opinions, assumptions and views that have emerged for them as they listen to the problem. It is designed to help the problem holder to listen better and to hear the story from 'between the lines'.

PRACTICE EXAMPLE

My problem was my relationship with a service user. There never seemed to be a satisfactory outcome from our meetings. Other colleagues had also reported the same problems and I just didn't know what to do next. Sitting outside the circle was very strange at first. I wanted to turn around and say, 'I have tried that' or 'Don't you think that I haven't considered that?' However, I was forced to listen, not stop the conversation, and the more I let go, the more I allowed the ideas in. I was listening acutely and it made me test myself as to what I had actually done before.

(Social worker)

Storytelling

Storytelling is a creative way of exploring the problem holder's issue. The problem holder is asked to tell the story in the third person and after questions from the group other set members tell stories of their own that they think have a connection to the problem holder's story. The stories are always true stories, and are the closest to participants offering advice or solutions.

PRACTICE EXAMPLE

My issue was a decision I had to take about taking up a new job – it was quite complex as it would involve family changes. I found it quite challenging talking about the issue in the third party; however, it was quite revealing in itself. I hadn't realised that I felt quite guilty about the opportunity when other colleagues were losing their jobs. It highlighted the important aspects for me. Listening to other people's stories of similar situations was interesting; they were not offering their story as the 'right way' but just something I might find helpful. It revealed some things I just had not considered about the long term and that I was not alone in having a problem like this.

(Social work manager)

Constellations

This method only works where the issue holder has a problem that involves complex organisational issues or where there are inter-relationship issues. The problem holder places other set members around the room in a constellation to represent the problem, for example, some close, some far away, some 'looking at' the problem, some 'looking away'. Each set member reports on how it feels to be where they have been positioned. The problem holder has the opportunity to change the positions and test the responses.

PRACTICE EXAMPLE

It was my first case that involved different agencies, drug abuse team, hospital services, housing, probation services and of course the social work team and I was struggling to understand the dynamics of the situation. The facilitator suggested this approach. One set member represented the client and I sat him on a chair in the middle of the room; others represented all the different agencies and his family. Some were very close, others looking away from the problem but close and others far away, yet this needed us all to work together. With the help of the group I arranged the agencies and family to form a circle around the client. I thought this is how I want it to be, all the services with the client in the middle. But the client said now he couldn't see anything outside the circle – no future of his own making. It really helped me re-evaluate the role of the agencies and what was needed from them to support the client.

(NQSW)

Developing yourself as a facilitator

The job of the action learning adviser, as described by Pedler and Abbott (2013), *is both ambitious and ambiguous, offering exciting opportunities but coming with few prescriptions about how best these can be accomplished.* The role of the facilitator has recently been under some scrutiny; indeed, the research work carried out by Pedler and Abbott (2008) was triggered by an action learning programme where facilitators were 'sacked' by set members, arguing that they were not 'doing it right'. This led indirectly to qualifications in action learning being developed. The commissioners of the programme, the NHS, put forward the argument that when employing action learning facilitators they had no benchmark for knowing whether facilitators could or would do it right and the qualifications in action learning facilitation were born. The challenge for those involved in action learning facilitator development is that it is arguably better learned than taught.

Table 9.2 illustrates three common approaches to developing as a set facilitator.

The first is how many people start, people who already have experience in the world that they operate in and have experience of being a set member starting to facilitate sets. This is often very successful particularly if the person has access to support.

The second is problematic in terms of quality control, the issue that was raised in the NHS case above, in that with many varieties of action learning from a direct intervention of the learning coach to more therapeutic models it is very difficult for a commissioning organisation to know what they are getting. Sometimes as with the Skills for Care programme the learning outcomes are mapped to the qualification standards and therefore participants can progress to full certification at a later stage.

The last stage is full qualification. Currently the only full qualification available is through Institute for Leadership and Management at level five and is offered by

Table 9.2 Three approaches to learning to be an action learning adviser

Approach	Description
1. Self-learning, self-development	Individual development of practice, not through a formally taught programme, but using observation, co-facilitation, coaching, reflective practice, reading, writing. Not validated by any external body
2. Proprietary or private training; usually via a taught programme based on a particular in-house model or approach to action learning	Usually focused on practical aspects of facilitation and methods of practice approved by the programme deliverer or client organisation May lead to in-house award, recognised by the awarding organisation, for example those of the World Institute of Action Learning and of Leadership in International Management May be quality-assured by an external body against the provider's own curriculum, e.g. as a development programme/endorsed by the Institute of Leadership and Management. May use logs of practice or mini case studies as evidence for satisfactory attendance and completion
3. Qualification recognised by a regulatory body; usually a taught programme, against a recognised framework or standard	Generally take a broader approach to understanding the different perspectives on action learning, coupled with critical reflection of own practice, and guided study of underpinning concepts and theory Formally assessed and accredited qualifications, e.g.: • Standards for action learning facilitators regulated by the Office of Qualifications and Examinations Regulation and as offered by the Institute for Leadership and Management • University-accredited programmes that map on to standards set by the UK Higher Education Academy

Adapted from Abbott and Boydell (2012).

Skills for Care for Social Workers. This qualification is regulated by the Office of Qualifications and Examining Regulations and operates to agreed standards.

CASE STUDY **9.1**

Skills for Care have used a combination of approaches to the development of action learning facilitators to support newly qualified social workers.

In the first phase (approach 2), an Institute for Leadership and Management quality-assured programme was delivered to 380 social workers and learning and development personnel across England. The programme was aligned to the standards and curriculum for the full qualification and focused on the 'in set' skills and processes in action learning and from which this chapter is based.

The second phase (approach 3) was for 70 of these participants to further their development by participating in the full certificate programme, which involved setting up action learning sets and evaluating the outcomes in both the set and the wider organisation. During the programme participants were encouraged to read widely about action learning both directly and indirectly through organisation development, reflective practice, for example. From this, participants were required to write up accounts of their practice – this is an important part of professional life because it encourages self-reflection and the integration of theory and practice. Some participants have published and are publishing these accounts in professional journals.

In the third phase (approach 1), action learning facilitator sets were encouraged and supported by external facilitation to get them started, and external resources of case studies were written and a video was made for the Skills for Care website. The facilitator sets help with all aspects of the facilitator's role and members challenge and support each other in their practice.

Finally, Skills for Care and the Centre for Action Learning Facilitation have developed a partnership to continue the training of facilitators through a community of practice. Those completing the certificate programme are invited to join the community of practice, as Lave and Wenger (1991) described, to be involved in action. That is, delivering introductory programmes, research, mentoring and support. This community of practice is one that brings all together to nurture both individual practice and the collective practice of action learning in social work by delivering introductory programmes, research and mentoring.

Chapter summary

- Facilitating action learning is a different process to teaching and training and supervision.

- The role of an action learning set facilitator is controversial, made especially so by the founder Revans's views. It is argued that there are three roles: the accoucheur, set facilitation and organisational development.

- The role of facilitation in the set is to help participants through the process of action learning and to support them to manage the process themselves.

- Crucial to the success of the action learning set is the pre-set preparation required to ensure the conditions are conducive to action learning.

- There are a number of processes that can be helpful in facilitating action learning that support the reflection and review of problems and challenges.

- Developing your role as a facilitator is crucial and there are opportunities to do this both informally and formally.

FURTHER READING

Abbott, C., Burtney, L. and Wall, C. (2014) Building capacity in social care: an evaluation of a national programme of action learning facilitator development, in Trehan, K. and Rigg, C. (eds) *Action Learning Research and Practice*. Taylor Francis: www.tandfonline.co.uk.

Pedler, M.J. and Abbott, C. (2013) *Action Learning Facilitation: A Practitioner's Guide*. Maidenhead, Berkshire: McGraw Hill.

References

Abbott, C. and Boydell, T. (2012) Learning to be an action learning facilitator: three approaches, in Pedler, M. (ed.) *Action Learning in Practice*, 4th edn. Farnham: Gower.

Adams, G.B. and Balfour, D.L. (2004) *Unmasking Administrative Evil*. New York: M.E. Sharpe.

Apps, J.W. (1985) *Improving Practice in Continuing Education: Modern Approaches for Understanding the Field and Determining Priorities*. San Francisco, CA: Jossey-Bass.

Argyris, C. and Schön, D. (1978) *Organisational Learning: A Theory of Action Perspective*. Reading: Addison Wesley.

Argyris, C. and Schön, D. (1996) *Organisational Learning*. Reading, MA: Addison-Wesley.

Association of Directors of Social Services (2002) *Press Release: Associations Voice Strong Concerns Over Community Care Bill* [online] Available at: www.nhsconfed.org/press/releases/ccbillconcerns.asp.

Attwood, M. (2007) Challenging from the margins to the main stream — improving renal services in a collaborative and entrepreneurial spirit. *Action Learning Research and Practice*, 4 (2): 191–198.

Banks, S. (1995) *Ethics and Values in Social Work*. Hampshire: Palgrave Macmillan.

Bannan-Ritland, B. (2003) The role of design in research: the integrative learning design framework. *Educational Researcher*, 32 (1): 21–24.

BASW (2013) *Employers' duty to protect social workers from burnout* [online] www.basw.co.uk/news/article/?id=330.

Bateson, G. (1972) *Steps to an Ecology of Mind: Collected Essays in Anthropology, Psychiatry, Evolution, and Epistemology*. Chicago, IL: University of Chicago Press.

Beaty, L., Bourner, T. and Frost, P. (1993) Action learning: reflections on becoming a set member. *Management Education and Development*, 24 (4): 350–367.

Bernard, J. and Goodyear, R. (1992) *Fundamentals of Clinical Supervision*. Boston, MA: Allyn and Bacon.

Berne, E. (1964) *Games People Play*. New York: Ballatine Books.

Boshyk, Y. and Dilworth, R.W. (eds) (2010) *Action Learning: History and Evolution*. Hampshire: Palgrave MacMillan.

Bourn, D. and Hafford-Letchfield, T. (2011) The role of social work professional supervision in conditions of uncertainty. *International Journal of Knowledge, Culture and Change Management*, 10 (9): 41–56.

Bradley, G. and Hojer, S. (2009) Supervision reviewed: reflections on two different social work models in England and Sweden. *European Journal of Social Work*, 12 (1): 71–85.

Brayne, H. and Carr, H. (2012) *Law for Social Workers*. Oxford: Oxford University Press.

Brockbank, A. and McGill, I. (2004) *The Action Learning Handbook: Powerful Techniques for Education*. Abingdon, Oxon: Professional Development and Training.

Brookfield, S.D. (1987) *Developing Critical Thinkers – Challenging Adults to Explore Alternative Ways of Thinking and Acting*. San Francisco, CA: Jossey-Bass.

Brookfield, S. (1994) Tales from the darkside: a phenomenology of adult critical reflection. *International Journal of Lifelong Education*, 13: 203–216.

Brown, H. (2011) The role of emotion in decision-making. *Journal of Adult Protection*, 13 (4): 194–202.

Brown, L., Tucker, C. and Domokos, T. (2003) Evaluating the impact of integrated health and social care teams on older people living in the community. *Health and Social Care in the Community*, 11 (2): 85–94.

Burke, B. and Dalrymple, J. (2000) Teamwork in multiprofessional care, in Payne, M. (ed.) *Teamwork in Multiprofessional Care*. Basingstoke: Palgrave Macmillan.

Butler-Sloss, Lord Justice E. (1988) *Report of the Inquiry into Child Abuse in Cleveland 1987*, cmnd 412. London: HMSO.

Carr, W. and Kemmis, S. (2009) Educational action research: a critical approach, in Noffke, S. and Somekh, B. (eds) *The Sage Handbook of Educational Action Research*. London: Sage, pp. 74–84.

Casey, D. (1976) The role of the set adviser, in Pedler, M. (ed.) *Action Learning in Practice*. Aldershot: Gower.

Casey, D. (2011) David Casey on the role of the set advisor, in Pedler, M. (ed.) *Action Learning in Practice*, 4th edn. Farnham: Gower Publishing.

Cheminais, R. (2009) *Effective Multi-Agency Partnerships: Putting Every Child Matters into Practice*. London: Sage.

The College of Social Work (2012) *PCF21 – Integrated Critical Reflective Practice* [online] www.tcsw.org.uk/uploadedFiles/TheCollege/Media_centre/PCF21Integrated CriticalReflectivePractice(1).pdf.

Commission for Social Care Inspection (2004) *Leaving Hospital: The Price of Delays*. London: Commission for Social Care Inspection.

Community Care Act (Delayed Discharges etc.) 2003. London: HMSO.

Corby, B. (2000) *Child Abuse: Towards a Knowledge Base*. Berkshire: Open University Press.

Dalrymple, J. and Burke, B. (1995) Some essential elements of anti-oppressive theory, in Dalrymple, J. and Burke, B. (eds) *Anti-Oppressive Practice: Social Care and the Law*. Buckingham: Open University Press.

Damasio, A. (2006) *Descartes' Error*. London: Picador Vintage.

D'Cruz, H., Gillingham, P. and Melendez, S. (2007) Reflexivity, its meanings and relevance for social work: a critical review of the literature. *British Journal of Social Work,* 37: 73–90.

Department of Health (1991) *Working Together to Safeguard Children*. London: The Stationery Office.

Dewey, J. (1933) *How We Think*. Boston, MA: DC Heath.

Dominelli, L. (1993) *Social Work: Mirror of Society or Its Conscience?* Sheffield: Department of Sociological Studies.

Dotlich, D.L. and Noel, J.L. (1998) *Action Learning: How the World's Top Companies Are Recreating Their Leaders and Themselves*. San Francisco, CA: Jossey-Bass.

Edmonstone, J. (2003) *The Action Learner's Toolkit*. Aldershot: Gower.

Equality Act (2010) c.15. London: HMSO.

French, J. and Raven, B. (1959) The bases of social power, in Cartwright, D. and Zander, A. (eds) *Group Dynamics*. New York: Harper & Row.

Gannon-Leary, P., Baines, S. and Wilson, R. (2006) Collaboration and partnership: a review and reflections on a national project to join up local services in England. *Journal of Interprofessional Care,* 20 (6): 665–674.

Gaunt, R. (1991) *Personal and Group Development for Managers: An Integrated Approach Through Action Learning*. Harlow: Longmans.

Glasby, J. (2003) *Hospital Discharge: Integrating Health and Social Care*. Abingdon: Radcliffe Medical Press.

Glendinning, C. (2003) Breaking down barriers: integrating health and care services for older people in England. *Health Policy,* 65 (2): 139–151.

Goleman, D. (1998) *Working with Emotional Intelligence*. London: Bloomsbury.

Gray, I., Field, R. and Brown, K. (2010) *Effective Leadership, Management and Supervision in Health and Social Care*. Exeter: Learning Matters.

Grint, K. (2005) Problems, problems, problems: the social construction of leadership. *Human Relations,* 58 (11): 1467–1494.

Grint, K. (2008) *Re-thinking D day*. Basingstoke: Palgrave Macmillan.

Habermas, J. (1979) What is universal pragmatics? in Habermas, J. (ed.) *Communication and the Evolution of Society*. Translated by T. McCarthy. London: Heinemann.

Hawkins, P. and Shohet, R. (2012) *Supervision in the Helping Professions*, 4th edn. Berkshire: Open University Press.

Healy, K. (2005) *Social Work Theories in Context: Creating Frameworks for Practice*. Basingstoke: Palgrave Macmillan.

Henwood, M. (2004) *Reimbursement and Delayed Discharges*. Leeds: Integrated Care Network.

Henwood, M., Hardy, B., Hudson, B. and Wistow, G. (1997) *Inter-agency Collaboration: Hospital and Continuing Care Sub-Study*. Leeds: Nuffield Institute for Health Community Division.

Horwarth, J. (2001) *The Child's World: Assessing Children in Need*. London: Jessica Kingsley.

House of Commons Select Committee (2002) *Delayed Discharges, Third Report of Session 2001–02*. HC 399–1. London: House of Commons Select Committee.

Howe, D. (2008) *The Emotionally Intelligent Social Worker*. Hampshire: Palgrave Macmillan.

Hudson, B. (2002) Interprofessionality in health and social care: the Achilles' heel of partnership? *Journal of Interprofessional Care,* 16 (1): 7–17.

International Association of School of Social Work (2001) *Statement of Ethical Principles* [online] www.ifsw.org/policies/statement-of-ethical-principles/.

International Federation of Social Workers (IFSW) (2002) *Definition of Social Work (in 16 languages)*. Berne, Switzerland: International Federation of Social Workers.

Janis, I. (1972) *Victims of Groupthink: A Psychological Study of Foreign Policy Decisions and Fiascoes*. Boston, MA: Houghton Mifflin.

Johnson, K. and Williams, I. (2007) *Managing Uncertainty and Change in Social Work and Social Care*. Lyme Regis: Russell House Publishing.

Kadushin, A. (1992) *Supervision in Social Work,* 3rd edn. New York: Columbia University Press.

Killon, J. and Todnew, G. (1991) A process of personal theory building. *Educational Leadership*, 48 (6): 14–16.

King, P.M. and Kitchener, K.S. (1994) *Developing Reflective Judgment: Understanding and Promoting Intellectual Growth and Critical Thinking in Adolescents and Adults*. San Francisco, CA: Jossey-Bass.

Kolb, D. (1984) *Experiential Learning: Experience as the Source of Learning and Development*. New Jersey: Prentice Hall.

Kramer, R. (2007) How might action learning be used to develop the emotional intelligence and leadership capacity of public administrators? *Journal of Public Affairs Education,* 13 (2): 205–242.

Lave, J. and Wenger, E. (1991) *Situated Learning: Legitimate Peripheral Participation*. Cambridge: Cambridge University Press.

Leary, M., Bodell, T., van Boeschoten, M. and Carlise, J. (1986) *The Qualities of Managing*. Sheffield: Training Agency.

Lewin, K. (1951) *Field Theory in Social Science: Selected Theoretical Papers*. Edited by D. Cartwright. Oxford: Harper & Row.

Lombard, D. (2009) *Support Shortfall Leaves Staff on the Brink of Burnout,* Community Care [online] www.communitycare.co.uk/articles/21/04/2009/111334/support-shortfall-leaves-staff-on-brink-of-burnout.htm.

London, M. (1997) *Job Feedback: Giving, Seeking and Using Feedback for Performance Improvement.* Mahwah, NJ: Lawrence Erlbaum.

Manthorpe, J. and Martineau, S. (2011) Serious case reviews in adult safeguarding in England: an analysis of a sample of reports. *British Journal of Social Work,* 41 (2): 224–241.

Marquardt, M. (2004) *Optimising the Power of Action Learning: Solving Problems and Building Leaders in Real Time.* Palo Alto, CA: Davies Black.

Marshall, J. (2001) Self-reflective inquiry practices, in Reason, P. and Bradbury, H. (eds) *Handbook of Action Research.* London: Sage.

Maslow A.H. (1969) *The Psychology of Science: A Reconnaissance.* Chicago, IL: Henry Reynery.

McGill, I. and Beaty, L. (2001) *Action Learning: A Guide for Professional Management and Educational Development,* 2nd edn. London: Kogan Page.

McGill, I. and Brockbank, A. (2006) *Facilitating Reflective Learning Through Mentoring and Coaching.* London: Kogan Page.

McLoughlin, H. and Thorpe, R. (1993) Action learning – a paradigm in emergence: the problems facing a challenge in traditional management development. *British Journal of Management,* 4 (1): 19–27.

Mead, G. (2006) Developing public service leaders through action inquiry, in Rigg, C. and Richards, S. (eds) *Action Learning, Leadership and Organisational Development in Public Services.* Abingdon: Routledge.

Menzies Lyth I. (1960) Social systems as a defence against anxiety. *Human Relations,* 13: 95–121.

Meyerson, D.E. (2003) *Tempered Radicals.* Boston, MA: Harvard Business School Press.

Mezirow, J. (1991) *Transformative Dimensions in Adult Learning.* San Francisco, CA: Jossey-Bass.

Morris, K. (2008) *Social Work and Multi-Agency Working: Making a Difference.* Bristol: The Policy Press.

Morrison, T. (2007) Emotional intelligence, emotion and social work: context, characteristics, complications and contribution. *British Journal of Social Work,* 37 (2): 245–263.

Mumford, A. (1995) Learning in action. *Industrial and Commercial Training,* 27 (8): 36–40.

Munro, E. (2011) *The Munro Review of Child Protection: Final Report: A Child Centred System.* London: TSO.

National Occupational Standards for Social Work (2002) *TOPSS UK Partnership.* Leeds: TOPSS.

Nicolini, D., Sher, M., Childerstone, S. and Gorli, M. (2004) In search of the structure that reflects: promoting organizational reflection practices in a UK health authority, in Reynolds, M. and Vince, R. (eds) *Organizing Reflection*. Aldershot: Ashgate Publishing.

Noble, C. and Irwin, J. (2009) Social work supervision: an exploration of the current challenges in a rapidly changing social, economic and political environment. *Journal of Social Work*, 9 (3): 345–358.

O'Connor, L., Cecil, B. and Boudioni, M. (2009) Preparing for practice: an evaluation of an undergraduate social work 'preparation for practice' module. *Social Work Education*, 28 (4): 436–454.

O'Hara, S., Bourner, T. and Webber, T. (2004) The practice of self managed action learning. *Action Learning: Research and Practice*, 1 (1): 29–42.

Okitikpi, T. (2011) *Social Control and the Use of Power in Social Work with Children and Families*. Lyme Regis: Russell House Publishing.

Paechter, C. (1998) *Educating the Other: Gender, Power and Schooling*. London: Falmer Press.

Payne, M. (2006) *What Is Professional Social Work?* Bristol: Policy Press.

Pedler, M.J. (1997) *Action Learning in Practice*, 3rd edn. Aldershot: Gower.

Pedler, M.J. (2008) *Action Learning for Managers*. Farnham: Gower.

Pedler, M.J. (2011) *Action Learning for Managers*. Farnham, Surrey: Gower.

Pedler, M.J. (2012) *Action Learning for Managers*. Hampshire: Gower Publishing.

Pedler, M.J. and Abbott, C. (2008) Am I doing it right? Facilitating action learning for service improvement. *Leadership in Health Services*, 21 (3): 185–199.

Pedler, M.J. and Abbott, C. (2013) *Facilitating Action Learning*. Berkshire: McGraw-Hill.

Pedler, M.J. and Aspinwall K. (1995) *Perfect PLC? The Purpose and Practice of Organizational Learning*. Maidenhead: McGraw-Hill Developing Organizations.

Pedler, M.J., Burgoyne, J. and Boydell, T. (2010) *A Manager's Guide to Leadership*. Berkshire: McGraw-Hill.

Pedler, M.J., Abbott, C., Brook, C. and Burgoyne, J. (2013) *Improving Social Work Practice Through Critically Reflective Action Learning*. Skills for Care [online] www.skillsforcare.org.uk.

Plsek, P. and Greenhalgh, T. (2004) The challenge of complexity in health care. *British Medical Journal*, 323 (7313): 625–658.

Pullen-Sansfaçon, A. and Ward, D. (2012) Making interprofessional working work: introducing a groupwork perspective. *British Journal of Social Work* [online] www.bjsw. oxfordjournals.org/content/early/2012/12/29/bjsw.bcs194.abstract.

Rabi, I.I. (1993) Great Minds Start With Questions in *Parents Magazine*.

Raelin, J.A. (2001) Public reflection as the basis of learning. *Management Learning*, 321: 11–30.

Raelin, J.A. (2008) Emancipatory discourses and liberation. *Management Learning*, 395: 519–540.

Reed, J. and Proctor, S. (1993) *Nurse Education: A Reflective Approach*. London: Edward Arnold.

Revans, R.W. (1971) *Developing Effective Managers*. New York: Praeger.

Revans, R. (1980) *Action Learning: New Techniques for Managers*. London: Blond and Briggs.

Revans, R.W. (1981) The nature of action learning. *Omega*, 9 (1): 9–24.

Revans, R.W. (1982) *The Origin and Growth of Action Learning*. London: Chartwell-Bratt.

Revans, R.W. (1983) *ABC of Action Learning*. Bromley: Chartwell-Bratt.

Revans, R.W. (1984) *Sequence of Managerial Achievement*. Bradford: MCB University Press.

Revans, R.W. (1988) *The Golden Jubilee of Action Learning: A Collection of Papers Written During 1988*. Manchester, UK: Manchester Business School, pp. 15–36.

Revans, R.W. (1998) *ABC of Action Learning*. London: Lemos and Crane.

Revans, R. (2011) *ABC of Action Learning*. Farnham: Gower.

Reynolds, M. (1998) Reflection and critical reflection in management learning. *Management Learning*, 29 (2): 183–200.

Reynolds, M. and Vince, R. (2004a) Critical management education and action-based learning: synergies and contradictions. *Academy of Management Learning and Education*, 3 (4): 442–456.

Reynolds, M. and Vince, R. (eds) (2004b) *Organising Reflection*. Aldershot: Ashgate Publishing.

Rittel, H.W.J. and Webber, M.M. (1973) Dilemmas in a general theory of planning. *Policy Science*, 4: 155–169.

Schön, D. (1973) *Beyond the Stable State: Public and Private Learning in a Changing Society*. Harmondsworth: Penguin.

Schön, D. (1983) *The Reflective Practitioner: How Professionals Think in Action*. New York: Basic Books.

Seebohm Report (1968) *Report of the Committee on Local Authority and Allied Personal Social Services*. London: HMSO.

Skills for Care and the Children's Workforce Development Council (2007) *Providing Effective Supervision*. Leeds: Skills for Care.

Smith, P.A.C. and O'Neil, J. (2003) A review of action learning literature 1994–2000. *Journal of Workplace Learning*, 15 (2): 63–69.

Smyth, J. (1989) Developing and sustaining critical reflection in teacher education. *Journal of Teacher Education*, 40 (2): 2–9.

Stoll, L., Fink, D. and Earl, L. (2003) *It's About Learning (and It's About Time): What's In It for Schools?* London: Routledge Falmer.

Stoltenberg, C. and Delworth, U. (1987) *Supervising Counselors and Therapists: A Developmental Approach.* San Francisco, CA: Jossey-Bass.

Strier, R. (2007) Anti-oppressive research in social work: a preliminary decision. *British Journal of Social Work,* 37 (5): 857–871.

Tait, L. and Lester, H. (2005) Encouraging user involvement in mental health services. *Advances in Psychiatric Treatment,* 11: 168–175.

The Children Act 2004 (c.31). London: HMSO.

Thompson, N. (1997) *Anti-discriminatory Practice,* 2nd edn. Basingstoke: Macmillan.

Thompson, N. (2009) *Promoting Equality, Valuing Diversity.* Lyme Regis: Russell House Publishing.

Thompson, N. (2012) Why we must reaffirm professionalism in social work [online] www.guardian.co.uk/social-care network/2012/apr/23/professional development-work-practices.

Trehan, K. (2011) Critical action learning, in Pedler, M. (ed.) *Action Learning in Practice,* 4th edn. Aldershot: Gower Publishing.

Trehan, K. and Pedler, M. (2010) Critical action learning, in Gold, J., Thorpe, R. and Mumford, A. (eds) *Gower Handbook of Management Development,* 5th edn. Farnham, Surrey: Gower.

Vince, R. (2002) Organizing reflection. *Management Learning,* 33 (5): 374–384.

Williams, S. and Rutter, L. (2010) *The Practice Educator's Handbook.* Exeter: Learning Matters.

Willmott, H. (1994) Management education: provocations to a debate. *Management Learning,* 25 (1): 105–106.

Willmott, H.C. (1997) Critical management learning, in Burgoyne, J. and Reynolds, M. (eds) *Management Learning.* London: Sage, pp. 161–176.

Woolgar, S. (1988) *Knowledge and Reflexivity: New Frontiers in the Sociology of Knowledge.* London: Sage.

Yorks, L., O'Neil, J. and Marsick, V.J. (eds) (1999) *Action Learning: Successful Strategies for Individual, Team and Organisational Development.* Baton Rouge, LA: Academy of HRD.

Zlotnik, J.L. (2002) Preparing social workers for child welfare practice: lessons from an historical review of the literature. *Journal of Health and Social Policy,* 14 (3 & 4): 5–21.

Index